WHAT'S THE DIFFERENCE?

WHAT'S THE
DIFFERENCE?

Manhood and Womanhood

Defined According to the Bible

STUDY GUIDE DEVELOPED BY DESIRING GOD

CROSSWAY BOOKS

WHEATON, ILLINOIS

What's the Difference?

Copyright © 2009 by Desiring God Foundation

Published by Crossway Books

   a publishing ministry of Good News Publishers
   1300 Crescent Street
   Wheaton, Illinois 60187

This study guide is based on and is a companion to *What's the Difference? Manhood and Womanhood Defined According to the Bible* (DVD) by John Piper (Crossway Books, 2009).

All rights reserved. No part of this publication may be reproduced, stored in a retrieval system, or transmitted in any form by any means, electronic, mechanical, photocopy, recording, or otherwise, without the prior permission of the publisher, except as provided for by USA copyright law.

Cover photo: Photos.com

First printing 2009

Printed in the United States of America

Unless otherwise indicated, Scripture quotations are from the ESV® Bible (*The Holy Bible, English Standard Version®*), copyright © 2001 by Crossway Bibles, a publishing ministry of Good News Publishers. Used by permission. All rights reserved.

Scripture quotations marked NASB are from *The New American Standard Bible.*® Copyright © The Lockman Foundation 1960, 1962, 1963, 1968, 1971, 1972, 1973, 1975, 1977, 1995. Used by permission.

Scripture references marked TNIV are from the Holy Bible, Today's New International® Version TNIV©. Copyright 2001, 2005 by International Bible Society®. Used by permission of International Bible Society®. All rights reserved worldwide.

"TNIV" and "Today's New International Version" are trademarks registered in the United States Patent and Trademark Office by International Bible Society®.

All emphases in Scripture quotations have been added by the author.

Trade paperback ISBN: 978-1-4335-0767-0

PDF ISBN: 978-1-4335-0768-7

Mobipocket ISBN: 978-1-4335-0769-4

CONTENTS

INTRODUCTION TO THIS STUDY GUIDE

THE TOPIC OF HUMAN SEXUALITY is as unavoidable as is our own sexual identity as male or female persons. What does it mean to be a man? What does it mean to be a woman? Are men and women equal? Are men and women different? Should men and women have distinctive roles within the family or within the church? These are questions in contemporary evangelicalism and in our society that need to be answered. The church cannot remain "neutral" on this issue; it must take a stand one way or another.

The issue is important for a number of reasons. Aside from the practical concerns for parenting, leading the church, relating in a marriage, and responding to homosexuality, the topic of human sexuality is tied to biblical authority and hermeneutics. Wayne Grudem explains:

> In the widely influential blog "Together for the Gospel," Mark Dever, senior pastor of Capitol Hill Baptist Church in Washington, DC, recently wrote:

"It is my best and most sober judgment that this position [egalitarianism] is effectively an undermining of—a breach in— the authority of Scripture. . . . It seems to me and others (many who are younger than myself) that *this issue of egalitarianism and complementarianism is increasingly acting as the watershed distinguishing those who will accommodate Scripture to culture, and those who will attempt to shape culture by Scripture.* You may disagree, but this is our honest concern before God. It is no lack of charity, nor honesty. It is no desire for power or tradition for tradition's sake. It is our sober conclusion from observing the last 50 years. . . .

Of course there are issues more central to the gospel than gender issues. However, *there may be no way the authority of Scripture is being undermined more quickly or more thoroughly in our day than through the hermeneutics of egalitarian readings of the Bible.* And when the authority of Scripture is undermined, the gospel will not long be acknowledged."[1]

Throughout this study guide you will have the opportunity to test Mark Dever's warning, as you will learn about egalitarianism and complementarianism and how each view seeks to support its understanding of masculinity and femininity.

Perhaps most importantly, however, the issue of manhood and womanhood, and male and female roles, is related to the glory of God. It is related to our joyful reflections of that glory, created in the image of God as male and female persons. Therefore, it is our hope that you will not only come to solid, biblical convictions on what it means to be a man or a woman, and a husband or a wife, but also that you will gladly live out this biblical vision to the glory of God.

This study guide is designed to be used in a twelve-session,[2] guided group study that focuses on the *What's the Difference?*

Manhood and Womanhood Defined According to the Bible DVD set.[3] After an introductory lesson, each subsequent lesson examines one 25-minute session[4] from *What's the Difference?* You, the learner, are encouraged to prepare for the viewing of each session by reading and reflecting upon Scripture, by considering key quotations, and by asking yourself penetrating questions. Your preparatory work for each lesson is marked with the heading "Before You Watch the DVD, Study and Prepare" in Lessons 2–11.

The workload is conveniently divided into five daily (and manageable) assignments. There is also a section suggesting further study. This work is to be completed individually before the group convenes to view the DVD and discuss the material.

> Throughout this study guide, paragraphs printed in a shaded box like this one are excerpts from a book written by John Piper (or, occasionally another author), or excerpts taken from the *Desiring God* Web site. They are included to supplement the study questions and to summarize key or provocative points.

The Last Battle

The second section in Lessons 2–11, entitled "Further Up and Further In," is designed for the learner who wants to explore the concepts and ideas introduced in the lesson in greater detail. This section is not required, but will deepen your understanding of the material.

The third section in Lessons 2–11, entitled "While You Watch the DVD, Take Notes," is to be completed as the DVD is playing. This section includes fill-in-the-blanks and leaves space for note-taking. You are encouraged to engage with the DVD by filling in the appropriate blanks and writing down other notes that will aid you in the group discussion.

The fourth section in each normal lesson is "After You Watch the DVD, Discuss What You've Learned." Three discussion questions are provided to guide and focus the conversation. You may record, in the spaces provided, notes that will help you contribute to the conversation. Or you may use this space to record things from the discussion that you want to remember.

The final section is an application section: "After You Discuss, Make Application." You will be challenged to record a "take-away point" and to engage in a certain activity that is a fitting response to the content presented in the lesson.

Group leaders will want to find the Leader's Guide, included at the end of this study guide, immediately.

Life transformation will only occur by the grace of God. Therefore, we highly encourage you to seek the Lord in prayer throughout the learning process. Pray that God would open your eyes to see wonderful things in his Word. Pray that he would grant you the insight and concentration you need in order to get the most from this resource. Pray that God would cause you not merely to understand the truth, but also to rejoice in it. And pray that the discussion in your group would be mutually encouraging and edifying. We've included objectives at the beginning of each lesson. These objectives won't be realized without the gracious work of God through prayer.

NOTES

1. Mark Dever, as quoted by Grudem in *Evangelical Feminism: A New Path to Liberalism?* (Wheaton, IL: Crossway, 2006), 18–19. See Grudem's footnote for the bibliographic information.

2. While this study guide is ideally suited for a twelve-session study, it is possible to complete it in six sessions. For instructions on how to use this study guide for a six-session group study, turn to Appendix A: Six-Session Intensive Option.

3. Although this resource is designed to be used in a group setting, it can also be used by the independent learner. Such a learner would have to decide how to use this resource in the most beneficial way. We would suggest doing everything but the group discussion, if possible.

4. Twenty-five minutes is only an approximation. Some sessions are longer; others are shorter.

LESSON 1

INTRODUCTION TO *WHAT'S THE DIFFERENCE? MANHOOD AND WOMANHOOD DEFINED ACCORDING TO THE BIBLE*

LESSON OBJECTIVES

It is our prayer that after you have finished this lesson . . .

> You will get a feel for how you and others in your group approach the issue of manhood and womanhood.

> Your curiosity would be roused, and questions would begin to come to mind.

> You will be eager to learn more about how you can live your life to the glory of God as a man or as a woman.

ABOUT YOURSELF

1) What is your name?

2) Tell the group something about yourself that they probably don't already know.

3) What are you hoping to learn from this group study?

A challenge in my view and a check on it.

A PREVIEW OF *WHAT'S THE DIFFERENCE?*

1) What conceptions does our culture have of what manhood and womanhood are? What stereotypes of manhood and womanhood do you see in movies, on television, in magazines, or on the internet? According to our culture, how does a man express his masculinity? How does a woman express her femininity?

F= bold, sexy, no fear, aggressive, cute/clutsy, capable
M= many women, strong, adventurous, smooth, romantic, confident

2) What, if anything, does the Christian church teach about manhood and womanhood? Do different churches communicate different messages about manhood and womanhood? If so, what are those different messages?

Anywhere from leadership from women to women don't do or say anything except care for the children.

LESSON 2
SETTING THE STAGE IN CULTURE: THE SECULAR
FEMINIST IMPULSE

A Companion Study to the What's the Difference? DVD,
Session 1

LESSON OBJECTIVES

It is our prayer that after you have finished this lesson . . .

› You will force yourself to think about definitions of manhood and womanhood.

› You will grow in discernment regarding our culture's influence on how we think about this subject.

› You will gladly reaffirm a commitment to letting the Bible have the final and determinative say on this subject.

BEFORE YOU WATCH THE DVD, STUDY AND PREPARE

DAY 1: WHAT IS MANHOOD?

In thinking about the sometimes complicated and confusing subject of biblical manhood and womanhood, it is important not to lose sight of how basic and relevant this subject really is. John Piper exposes how important it is to define manhood in an understandable way when he imagines the question of a little boy: "Dad, what does it mean to be a man and not a woman?"[1]

*QUESTION 1: If your son, or another little boy, asked *you* this question, how would you answer him?[2]

It means to be a leader, a protector, and a provider.

A lot of energy is being expended today minimizing the distinctions of manhood and womanhood. But we do not hear very often what manhood and womanhood *should* incline us to do. We are adrift in a sea of confusion over sexual roles. And life is not the better for it.[3]

Notice that the little boy's question is Question A and *not* Question B.

Question A: "Dad, what does it mean to be a man and not a woman?"

Question B: "Dad, what does it mean to be a man?"

QUESTION 2: Why are the last four words of Question A important? How might the answer to Question A be different than the answer to Question B?

Question A is asking more what the women shouldn't be.
Question B could have answers that are true of women as well

DAY 2: MANHOOD ACCORDING TO OUR CULTURE

Our culture, infected as it is by sin, tends to portray men at one of two extremes. John Piper explains:

> When sin entered the world, it ruined the harmony of marriage NOT because it brought headship and submission into existence, but because it twisted man's humble, loving headship into <u>hostile domination</u> in some men and <u>lazy indifference</u> in others.[4]

QUESTION 3: Which caricature of manhood is more commonly portrayed in our culture—hostile domination or lazy indifference? Which caricature do you think is more commonly embodied?

lazy indifference – seen in countless TV shows (in the US.)
hostile domination is seen more worldwide embodied.

Even though men are often portrayed in these ways, it is probable that most people in our culture recognize that men should not be either abusive or lazy. Deep down they know that there is a better way. Study Genesis 1:26–27 and Romans 2:14–15.

GENESIS 1:26–27

²⁶ Then God said, "Let us make man in our image, after our likeness. And let them have dominion over the fish of the sea and over the birds of the heavens and over the livestock and over all the earth and over every creeping thing that creeps on the

earth." ²⁷ So God created man in his own image, in the image of
God he created him; male and female he created them.

ROMANS 2:14–15

¹⁴ *For when Gentiles, who do not have the law, by nature do*
what the law requires, they are a law to themselves, even though
they do not have the law. ¹⁵ *They show that the work of the law*
is written on their hearts, while their conscience also bears wit-
ness, and their conflicting thoughts accuse or even excuse them.

*QUESTION 4: In light of these verses, do you think that
men and women should have a deep-rooted sense of true masculinity and femininity based on how God created them and the
"natural law"? Explain your answer.

yes - both male + female (even unbelievers)
were made in God's image
by nature men + women often have
leadership and submissive personalities
even when they don't know the Lord

> Distinctions in masculine and feminine roles are ordained
> by God as part of the created order, and should find an
> echo in every human heart.[5]

DAY 3: WHAT IS WOMANHOOD?

In Day 1, we considered a question that a little boy might ask
his father about manhood. Now consider the question of the
little girl: "Mom, what does it mean to be a woman and not a
man?"[6]

*QUESTION 5: If your daughter, or another little girl, asked *you* this question, how would you answer her?

Role: soothing, loving, peacemaking caregiver, the helper

QUESTION 6: What might be the long-term result if Christians had no answer to the little girl's question? What might happen if Christians told their sons and daughters that there is no essential difference between men and women?

- Men + women would not compliment each other. Therefore their effectiveness for the kingdom would be deminished.
- Breakdown of the family

DAY 4: WOMANHOOD ACCORDING TO OUR CULTURE

The National Organization for Women (NOW) was established in 1966. According to the NOW web site (www.now.org), "NOW is the largest, most comprehensive feminist advocacy group in the United States. Our purpose is to take action to bring women into full participation in society—sharing equal rights, responsibilities and opportunities with men, while living free from discrimination." It has "500,000 contributing members and 550 chapters in all 50 states and the District of Columbia."

QUESTION 7: What encounters have you had with modern-day feminism? What does feminism teach about womanhood?

- Men + women are the same. They should be equal with men.

- sister-in-laws desire for recognition, respect, capability

Two prominent female figures in American culture are Britney Spears and Hillary Clinton. They represent two very different visions of womanhood.

*QUESTION 8: In the two columns below, list characteristics of these two women as they are portrayed by the media. What might this exercise tell us about how womanhood is depicted in our culture?

Britney Spears	Hillary Clinton
-sexually -pushing the boundaries -idol -power over men through body	-power + authority -equal playing field with men -power over men through mind

DAY 5: HUMAN SEXUALITY AND BIBLICAL AUTHORITY

Having briefly considered what our culture thinks about biblical manhood and womanhood, we need to make explicit an assumption that runs throughout this entire study guide: the final authority on human sexuality, masculinity and femininity, and male and female roles in the home and in the church is the written Word of God, the Bible. We must state this up front because all too often cultural opinions or our own subjective judgments about what's "beautiful" or "fair" carry more weight than Scripture. Piper offers us a warning and an exhortation:

> There's no point in just talking about what people think about manhood and what people think about womanhood, because there are a thousand thoughts and a thousand opinions in the world. What really matters is what God thinks about manhood and womanhood—what God appointed for maleness and femaleness. That's the only thing that matters in the end. Other things may seem, in the short run, attractive, but they will leave you in pain at the end if they are not of God.[7]

QUESTION 9: According to Piper, how does joy relate to human sexuality?

There's joy in defining yourself by what the Bible says.

*QUESTION 10: Respond to the following statement: "Why should we believe what the Bible says about human sexuality? So many advances have been made in society and science since the Bible was written. And we all know that the Bible was written by men who lived in a male-dominated culture. So why should we listen to the Bible on this subject?"

It is the inherrent word of God that trascends culture. *How would I God is bigger than combat someone culture. who disagreed with this?

21

FURTHER UP AND FURTHER IN

Note: The "Further Up and Further In" section is for those who want to study more. It is a section for further reference and going deeper. The phrase "further up and further in" is borrowed from C. S. Lewis.

Read "Building Our Lives on the Bible," an online sermon at the Desiring God Web site.

QUESTION 11: According to Piper, what is the conservative impulse in Christianity? What is the liberal impulse?

QUESTION 12: How does this sermon relate to our study of biblical manhood and womanhood?

Listen to "Manhood, Womanhood, and God, Part 4," an online conference message by John Piper at the Desiring God Web site.[8]

Examine 2 Timothy 4:3–4.

2 TIMOTHY 4:3–4

> [3] *For the time is coming when people will not endure sound teaching, but having itching ears they will accumulate for them-*

selves teachers to suit their own passions, ⁴ and will turn away from listening to the truth and wander off into myths.

QUESTION 13: According to Piper, how does this passage relate to the issue of biblical manhood and womanhood?

QUESTION 14: Does strength of conviction equal arrogance? Defend your answer.

MATTHEW 10:24–31

> ²⁴ *A disciple is not above his teacher, nor a servant above his master. ²⁵ It is enough for the disciple to be like his teacher, and the servant like his master. If they have called the master of the house Beelzebul, how much more will they malign those of his household. ²⁶ So have no fear of them, for nothing is covered that will not be revealed, or hidden that will not be known. ²⁷ What I tell you in the dark, say in the light, and what you hear whispered, proclaim on the housetops. ²⁸ And do not fear those who kill the body but cannot kill the soul. Rather fear him who can destroy both soul and body in hell. ²⁹ Are not two sparrows sold for a penny? And not one of them will fall to the ground apart from your Father. ³⁰ But even the hairs of your head are all numbered. ³¹ Fear not, therefore; you are of more value than many sparrows.*

QUESTION 15: What examples does Piper present of "shrewd" and "politically correct" messages? Can you think of other similar examples from your own experience?

WHILE YOU WATCH THE DVD, TAKE NOTES
2 Timothy 3:14–17 (cf. 1:5)

- Continue in what you have learned from those who taught you

What was Ruth Piper like? What kind of mother and wife was she?

- very competent
- did everything when dad was away, but sat back and let dad read when he was back

What is sexual complementarity?

coming together of a man and woman to complement or complete each other

"I grew up in a home where I knew my mother's __submission__ was not based on lack of __competency__

How are the words "gender" and "sex" used?

gender = social/cultural

sex = biological

The assumption of contemporary feminism: Maleness and femaleness, at the root level of _____, are negligible realities.

AFTER YOU WATCH THE DVD, DISCUSS WHAT YOU'VE LEARNED

1) Think of a man in your life who exhibits true masculinity. What is it about him that makes him truly masculine? Then think of a woman in your life who exhibits true femininity. What is it about her that makes her truly feminine?

2) Was biblical manhood and womanhood modeled in the home in which you grew up? If so, in what ways?

3) How deep do the distinctions between men and women go? Are manhood and womanhood at the core of personhood? Or are they superficial and artificial constructions of culture? Or are they something in between?

AFTER YOU DISCUSS, MAKE APPLICATION

1) What was the most meaningful part of this lesson for you? Was there a sentence, concept, or idea that really struck you? Why? Record your thoughts in the space below.

2) Think about ways in which you express your masculinity or femininity. Make a list of masculine or feminine behaviors, thoughts, speech, attitudes, and roles that you have adopted. Are these expressions of your sexuality healthy and biblical?

NOTES

1. This question is reproduced from John Piper, "A Vision of Biblical Complementarity: Manhood and Womanhood Defined According to the Bible," in *Recovering Biblical Manhood and Womanhood: A Response to Evangelical Feminism*, eds. John Piper and Wayne Grudem (Wheaton, IL: Crossway, 2006), 33. The book *Recovering Biblical Manhood and Womanhood* is available for free in its entirety at the Web site of the Council on Biblical Manhood and Womanhood (www.cbmw.org). Please note that the first chapter of this book is also published separately as the book *What's the Difference?*

2. Questions marked with an asterisk (*) are questions that we deem to be particularly significant. If your group is completing this study using the six-session intensive option, we recommend that you complete these questions first and then, if time permits, complete the remaining questions. For more information, see Appendix A: Six-Session Intensive Option.

3. John Piper, "A Vision of Biblical Complementarity," 33.

4. John Piper, "Husbands Who Love Like Christ and the Wives Who Submit to Them," an online sermon at the Desiring God Web site (www.desiringGod.org). Throughout this study guide, articles and sermons at the Desiring God web site may be found by performing a Title Search on the home page.

5. This is the second affirmation of the Danvers Statement, which is published as Appendix 2 of *Recovering Biblical Manhood and Womanhood*. It can also be found at the Council on Biblical Manhood and Womanhood (CBMW) Web site.

6. This question is reproduced from John Piper, "A Vision of Biblical Complementarity," 33.

7. John Piper "Manhood, Womanhood, and God, Part 3," an online conference message at the Desiring God Web site.

8. This is a conference message available online at the Desiring God Web site.

LESSON 3
SETTING THE STAGE IN THE CHURCH: THE TRAGEDY OF FEMINIST AGNOSTICISM

A Companion Study to the What's the Difference? DVD, Session 2

LESSON OBJECTIVES

It is our prayer that after you have finished this lesson . . .

> You will be able to define the terms "evangelical feminism" and "complementarianism."

> You will grasp some of the social effects of feminism.

> You will perceive the need for clear definitions of masculinity and femininity.

BEFORE YOU WATCH THE DVD, STUDY AND PREPARE

DAY 1: MANHOOD AND WOMANHOOD ACCORDING TO THE CHURCH

In the previous lesson we considered how masculinity and femininity were portrayed and lived out in our culture. In this lesson we will consider how the church has handled human sexuality.

*QUESTION 1: What teachings have you heard about manhood and womanhood in the church? Record anything you can remember from sermons you've heard, Christian books you've read, or conversations you've had with other Christians.

women shouldn't teach men, in example at church, sister in law pursuing ordination, females in chapel services

TITUS 2:2–6

> [2] Older men are to be sober-minded, dignified, self-controlled, sound in faith, in love, and in steadfastness. [3] Older women likewise are to be reverent in behavior, not slanderers or slaves to much wine. They are to teach what is good, [4] and so train the young women to love their husbands and children, [5] to be self-controlled, pure, working at home, kind, and submissive to their own husbands, that the word of God may not be reviled. [6] Likewise, urge the younger men to be self-controlled.

QUESTION 2: According to these verses, do you think the church has an obligation to teach what manhood and womanhood are to the next generation? Explain.

yes : wise older people in the church to teach one on one, wisdom of pastors

DAY 2: EVANGELICAL FEMINISM

The modern American church's stance toward human sexuality and male and female roles can be described by two basic approaches. The first may be called "evangelical feminism." Here is a rough description of this first approach:

Evangelical Feminism: A view shared by evangelical Christians who believe that God has not assigned different roles to men and women within marriage and the church. In this view, men and women share a joint authority and responsibility before God for leadership. Men and women are both qualified to serve as elders within the church.[1] (This study guide will use "evangelical feminism" and "egalitarianism" synonymously.)

It is important to realize that evangelical feminism, especially in its advocacy for women preaching pastors, is a new development within church history. Wayne Grudem explains:

For the first eighteen hundred years of the history of the church, women played influential roles in evangelism, prayer, ministries of mercy, writing, financial support, political influence, private exhortation and encouragement and counsel, and teaching of women and children. But they never became pastors of churches, and rarely did they speak or teach publicly in mixed assemblies of men and women. When women did preach or teach the Bible to men, it was generally in "sectarian" movements such as the Quakers.[2]

QUESTION 3: Do you know anyone who would consider themselves an "evangelical feminist"? If so, how have they talked about this issue of human sexuality?

yes – sister-in-law
definitions in Bible were culturally
irrelevant

The major organization promoting evangelical feminism is Christians for Biblical Equality (CBE). Their web site is www. cbeinternational.org. Here is how this organization defines itself:

> **Christians for Biblical Equality** is a nonprofit organization comprised of individual and church members from more than 100 denominations who believe that the Bible, properly interpreted, teaches the fundamental equality of men and women of all ethnicities and all economic classes, based on the teachings of Scripture as reflected in Galatians 3:28: "There is neither Jew nor Gentile, neither slave nor free, neither male nor female, for you are all one in Christ Jesus" (TNIV).[3]

*QUESTION 4: Can you detect anything in this statement that might be misleading or potentially manipulative? Explain.

properly interpreted =
Who determines that?

DAY 3: COMPLEMENTARIANISM

The second basic approach to human sexuality and roles can be called "complementarianism." Here is a rough description of this second approach:

> **Complementarianism:** A view shared by evangelical Christians who believe that God has assigned different and complementary roles to men and women within marriage and the church. In this view, men bear a unique authority and responsibility before God for leadership. Only men are qualified to serve as elders within the church.[4]

*QUESTION 5: Do you know anyone who would consider themselves a "complementarian"? If so, how have they talked about this issue of human sexuality?

men are leaders in home
women submit to husbands

The major organization promoting complementarianism is the Council on Biblical Manhood and Womanhood (CBMW). Their web site is www.cbmw.org. Here is how this organization describes itself:

> In 1987, a group of pastors and scholars assembled to address their concerns over the influence of feminism not only in our culture but also in evangelical churches. Because of the widespread compromise of biblical understanding of manhood and womanhood and its tragic effects on the

home and the church, these men and women established The Council on Biblical Manhood and Womanhood.

In opposition to the growing movement of feminist egalitarianism they articulated what is now known as the complementarian position which affirms that men and women are equal in the image of God, but maintain complementary differences in role and function. In the home, men lovingly are to lead their wives and family as women intelligently are to submit to the leadership of their husbands. In the church, while men and women share equally in the blessings of salvation, some governing and teaching roles are restricted to men.[5]

QUESTION 6: How is this self-description from the CBMW different from the way that CBE defines themselves?

CBMW = working more defensively
CBE = quotes scripture

This study guide will argue for the complementarian perspective on manhood and womanhood as the biblical one. Throughout the study guide we will attempt to represent the egalitarian perspective fairly, but it is not our intention to provide a neutral overview (or an exhaustive defense) of both sides. In future lessons we will rather concentrate on inductive Bible study of the key biblical passages.

DAY 4: STATEMENTS FROM EGALITARIANS

When presenting a particular perspective, it is important to represent that perspective fairly. One of the best ways to do this is to quote the best advocates of that perspective. Therefore, here are two statements made by prominent evangelical feminists concerning human sexuality:

> Gretchen Gabelein Hull writes, "Biblical feminists lovingly ask the Christian community to abandon artificial role playing and to be sex blind in assessing each individual's qualifications for ministry" (*Equal to Serve*, p. 128).
>
> And Mary Stewart Van Leeuwen expresses her confidence that the Bible's "main thrust is toward the leveling, not the maintenance, of birth-based status differences" (*Gender and Grace*, p. 235)."[6]

*QUESTION 7: What do these statements imply about those who disagree with the evangelical feminist position?

—beliefs are artificial
—need for more open interpretation

QUESTION 8: If you were arguing for the complementarian position, how might you respond to Hull and Van Leeuwen's statements?

—What makes it "artifial"?
—where in the Bible does it say to do these things?

DAY 5: THE SOCIAL RESULTS OF BEING "SEX BLIND"

The debate between evangelical feminists and complementarians is not merely academic. At root, the debate concerns our sexual identity and our understanding of how God made us and how he wants us to behave toward the opposite sex. Confusion about our sexuality and sexual roles will inevitably have social consequences. This is apparent from how our own culture has changed in the last few decades as a result of the rise of feminism.

*QUESTION 9: What social results have you observed as our culture has embraced the feminist perspective?

- more women working
- decrease of traditional family structure (women feel liberated in being able to get a divorce)
- women having babies alone
- weaker men, less expectation on them

Now look at Deuteronomy 24:5; Joshua 1:14–15; and Nahum 3:5, 12–13.

DEUTERONOMY 24:5

> [5] When a man is newly married, he shall not go out with the army or be liable for any other public duty. He shall be free at home one year to be happy with his wife whom he has taken.

JOSHUA 1:14–15

> [14] Your wives, your little ones, and your livestock shall remain in the land that Moses gave you beyond the Jordan, but all the men of valor among you shall pass over armed before your brothers and shall help them, [15] until the LORD gives rest to your brothers as he has to you, and they also take possession of the land that the LORD your God is giving them. . . .

NAHUM 3:5, 12–13

> [5] *Behold, I am against you, declares the* LORD *of hosts, and will lift up your skirts over your face; and I will make nations look at your nakedness and kingdoms at your shame. . . .* [12] *All your fortresses are like fig trees with first-ripe figs—if shaken they fall into the mouth of the eater.* [13] *Behold, your troops are women in your midst. The gates of your land are wide open to your enemies; fire has devoured your bars.*

✱ QUESTION 10: In light of these verses, how should a Christian respond to women serving in active combat in the military?

FURTHER UP AND FURTHER IN

Read the Rationale Section of the Danvers Statement (below).

The Danvers Statement was written in 1987 as the charter statement of the Council on Biblical Manhood and Womanhood. John Piper will review the Affirmations section of this statement in the next lesson, but we wanted to provide you an opportunity in this lesson to read the opening section. We have inserted study questions after each two points of rationale. There are ten total points to the Rationale section.

Rationale

We have been moved in our purpose by the following contemporary developments which we observe with deep concern:

1) The widespread uncertainty and confusion in our culture

regarding the complementary differences between masculinity and femininity;

2) the tragic effects of this confusion in unraveling the fabric of marriage woven by God out of the beautiful and diverse strands of manhood and womanhood;

QUESTION 11: Does confusion over manhood and womanhood really unravel the "fabric of marriage"? Defend your answer.

3) the increasing promotion given to feminist egalitarianism with accompanying distortions or neglect of the glad harmony portrayed in Scripture between the loving, humble leadership of redeemed husbands and the intelligent, willing support of that leadership by redeemed wives;

4) the widespread ambivalence regarding the values of motherhood, vocational homemaking, and the many ministries historically performed by women;

QUESTION 12: Is motherhood and vocational homemaking valued by our culture or by feminism? Is it valued in the Bible? Cite examples and biblical passages to support your answer.

5) the growing claims of legitimacy for sexual relationships which have Biblically and historically been considered illicit or perverse, and the increase in pornographic portrayal of human sexuality;

6) the upsurge of physical and emotional abuse in the family;

QUESTION 13: Does the issue of biblical manhood and womanhood have any bearing on homosexuality, pornography, or domestic abuse? If so, explain how.

7) the emergence of roles for men and women in church leadership that do not conform to Biblical teaching but backfire in the crippling of Biblically faithful witness;

8) the increasing prevalence and acceptance of hermeneutical oddities devised to reinterpret apparently plain meanings of Biblical texts;

QUESTION 14: How might the debate about sexual roles impact the church's doctrine of Scripture?

9) the consequent threat to Biblical authority as the clarity of Scripture is jeopardized and the accessibility of its meaning

to ordinary people is withdrawn into the restricted realm of technical ingenuity;

10) and behind all this the apparent accommodation of some within the church to the spirit of the age at the expense of winsome, radical Biblical authenticity which in the power of the Holy Spirit may reform rather than reflect our ailing culture.

QUESTION 15: According to this statement, what should a Christian's relationship to culture look like?

WHILE YOU WATCH THE DVD, TAKE NOTES

Jewett's admission: "_Sexuality_ permeates one's individual being to its very depth; it conditions every facet of one's life as a _person_."

Jewett's breathtaking ignorance

we are man or woman to our core, but we don't know what that means.

"Egalitarian" and "Complementarian"

Egalitarian = what you are by natur does not determine your qualification

Piper's parenthesis on the use of language

Gretchen Hull's language is manipulative
"artificial role playing" = she's not
allowing a middle ground, she's making
the opponent sound greatly extreme

Piper's soapbox

There is a reason why God asked Adam
first where he was in the garden. Women
in war shows the decline of chivalry.

James Dobson: "Feminist resistance to making man hood
and womanhood significant in behavior and role determination
is partner to some of the most painful social and spiritual issues
of our day."

The need for definitions of masculinity and femininity.

Social problems find their
root in our failure to recognize
our unique roles,

AFTER YOU WATCH THE DVD, DISCUSS WHAT YOU'VE LEARNED

1) Do you agree with Jewett's agnosticism concerning what true masculinity and femininity are? Does the Bible have anything to teach us about manhood and womanhood?

2) Piper accuses two evangelical feminists of being manipulative in their use of language and then invites correction if his audience observes him being manipulative in his use of language. Do you think that Piper is clear and that he fairly presents the alternatives in this session?

3) Why does Piper get so upset about women serving in active combat in the military? Is it because he thinks that women are unable to fight?

AFTER YOU DISCUSS, MAKE APPLICATION

1) What was the most meaningful part of this lesson for you? Was there a sentence, concept, or idea that really struck you? Why? Record your thoughts in the space below.

2) In a heated debate, such as this one over sexual roles, Christians are obligated to speak the truth in love to the glory of God. Therefore, compose your own resolve about how you will act and speak in this debate. You may include your commitment to do the following: to listen carefully; to understand a position before critiquing it; to represent those who disagree with you fairly; to argue without making fallacies; to show proper and controlled emotions; etc. Then share your resolve with someone else.

NOTES

1. This definition is reproduced from *Male and Female He Created Them: A Study on Biblical Manhood and Womanhood*, which is a curriculum designed by *The Bethlehem Institute*, a ministry of Bethlehem Baptist Church (www.thebethleheminstitute.org).

2. Grudem, *Evangelical Feminism and Biblical Truth* (Sisters, OR: Multnomah, 2004), 460.

3. This quotation is taken from the "About CBE" webpage (www.cbe international.org/new/about/about_cbe.shtml, accessed November 12, 2008).

4. This definition is also reproduced from the curriculum *Male and Female He Created Them*.

5. This quotation is taken from the "About Us" webpage (www.cbmw. org/About-Us, accessed November 12, 2008).

6. Both quotations are taken from the notes to the Sexual Complementarity seminar, which is available online at the Desiring God Web site.

LESSON 4
RECOVERING BIBLICAL MANHOOD AND
WOMANHOOD

*A Companion Study to the What's the Difference? DVD,
Session 3*

LESSON OBJECTIVES

It is our prayer that after you have finished this lesson . . .

> › You will be able to explain how men and women are
>   equal.
> › You will be able to describe the complementarian posi-
>   tion in broad terms.
> › You will grapple with Piper's definitions of masculinity
>   and femininity.

BEFORE YOU WATCH THE DVD, STUDY AND PREPARE

DAY 1: CREATED EQUALLY IN THE IMAGE
OF GOD

Most of this study guide will explore ways in which men and
women are different and are called to different, though comple-

mentary, roles. Before exploring the differences, however, we should begin by asserting the foundational equality of men and women. This will hopefully prevent misunderstandings when we turn to how men and women are different.

It will be crucial to remember throughout this study that:

A man's call to leadership does not imply that he is thereby superior to a woman; likewise, a woman's call to submission does not imply that she is thereby inferior to a man.

Let's start by reading Genesis 1:26–28.

GENESIS 1:26–28

> [26] Then God said, "Let us make man in our image, after our likeness. And let them have dominion over the fish of the sea and over the birds of the heavens and over the livestock and over all the earth and over every creeping thing that creeps on the earth." [27] So God created man in his own image, in the image of God he created him; male and female he created them. [28] And God blessed them. And God said to them, "Be fruitful and multiply and fill the earth and subdue it and have dominion over the fish of the sea and over the birds of the heavens and over every living thing that moves on the earth."

*QUESTION 1: Underline every phrase in this passage which applies equally to men and women.

QUESTION 2: Why might it be important to begin our study of biblical manhood and womanhood by stressing the ways in which men and women are equals?

— finding commonality
— relating to own another
— both identity is in God
— both valued by God

DAY 2: VALUED EQUALLY AS MEN AND WOMEN

Throughout the Old Testament we find that men and women should be equally valued as persons created in the image of God. One of the most well-known passages that honors women (and specifically, wives) is Proverbs 31.

Read again some of the verses in Proverbs 31 that describe the excellent wife.

PROVERBS 31:10–12, 25–31

> [10] *An excellent wife who can find? She is far more precious than jewels.* [11] *The heart of her husband trusts in her, and he will have no lack of gain.* [12] *She does him good, and not harm, all the days of her life.* . . . . [25] *Strength and dignity are her clothing, and she laughs at the time to come.* [26] *She opens her mouth with wisdom, and the teaching of kindness is on her tongue.* [27] *She looks well to the ways of her household and does not eat the bread of idleness.* [28] *Her children rise up and call her blessed; her husband also, and he praises her:* [29] *"Many women have done excellently, but you surpass them all."* [30] *Charm is deceitful, and beauty is vain, but a woman who fears the LORD is to be praised.* [31] *Give her of the fruit of her hands, and let her works praise her in the gates.*

QUESTION 3: Which of the following statements best describes the tone of this passage? If none of these statements capture what you think the tone is, offer your own suggestion.

a) Demeaning: The author of this passage clearly did not think a woman's work was equally valuable to what a man can do.

b) Apathetic: The author of this passage was mostly indifferent to the accomplishments of wives and mothers.

c) Exuberant: The author of this passage rejoices in what an excellent wife can do and how she fears the Lord.

d) Sarcastic: The author of this passage pretends to praise women but is only doing so in order to keep them suppressed.

Sometimes I feel in some men, there is a hint of D

One of the most powerful witnesses to the equal value and dignity of men and women was the way in which Jesus ministered to both men and women. It is true that in some ways Jesus' behavior toward women was countercultural in the first century and elevated them to a position of personal worth equal to that of men.

JOHN 4:25–30

> ²⁵ *The woman said to him, "I know that Messiah is coming (he who is called Christ). When he comes, he will tell us all things."* ²⁶ *Jesus said to her, "I who speak to you am he."* ²⁷ *Just then his disciples came back. They marveled that he was talking with a woman, but no one said, "What do you seek?" or, "Why are you talking with her?"* ²⁸ *So the woman left her water jar and went away into town and said to the people,* ²⁹ *"Come, see a*

man who told me all that I ever did. Can this be the Christ?"
30 They went out of the town and were coming to him.

LUKE 10:38–42

38 Now as they went on their way, Jesus entered a village. And a woman named Martha welcomed him into her house. 39 And she had a sister called Mary, who sat at the Lord's feet and listened to his teaching. 40 But Martha was distracted with much serving. And she went up to him and said, "Lord, do you not care that my sister has left me to serve alone? Tell her then to help me." 41 But the Lord answered her, "Martha, Martha, you are anxious and troubled about many things, 42 but one thing is necessary. Mary has chosen the good portion, which will not be taken away from her."

*QUESTION 4: Can either of these passages be used to prove that Jesus did not see any distinctions between men and women, or that Jesus intended women to be preaching pastors within the church?

I believe it communicates that women are important to the ministry and that Jesus felt it important that they learned about him. But, I don't see it saying that they should be pastors

DAY 3: REDEEMED EQUALLY FOR THE BLESSINGS OF SALVATION

One Scripture text that we will look at again in Lesson 11 is Galatians 3:28. This is perhaps the verse that is most often quoted by evangelical feminists in defense of their position. Though we believe that evangelical feminists misuse this verse, it is important to appreciate the positive message this verse does send.

Study Galatians 3:28 in the context of Galatians 3:23–29.

GALATIANS 3:23–29

> [23] *Now before faith came, we were held captive under the law, imprisoned until the coming faith would be revealed.* [24] *So then, the law was our guardian until Christ came, in order that we might be justified by faith.* [25] *But now that faith has come, we are no longer under a guardian,* [26] *for in Christ Jesus you are all sons of God, through faith.* [27] *For as many of you as were baptized into Christ have put on Christ.* [28] *There is neither Jew nor Greek, there is neither slave nor free, there is no male and female, for you are all one in Christ Jesus.* [29] *And if you are Christ's, then you are Abraham's offspring, heirs according to promise.*

QUESTION 5: Answering from the broader context, to what kind of equality is Galatians 3:28 testifying? In other words, in what way was Paul claiming that men and women are equal in this passage?

They had an equal blessing of ridding themselves of the law and becoming heirs of God through the death of Christ.

Another verse that we will revisit later makes the point crystal clear.

Consider 1 Peter 3:7 and Ephesians 3:4–6.

1 PETER 3:7 (NASB)

> [7] *You husbands in the same way, live with your wives in an understanding way, as with someone weaker, since she is a woman; and*

show her honor as a fellow heir [Greek: sugklāronomos] of the grace of life, so that your prayers will not be hindered.

EPHESIANS 3:4–6 (NASB)

⁴ By referring to this, when you read you can understand my insight into the mystery of Christ, ⁵ which in other generations was not made known to the sons of men, as it has now been revealed to His holy apostles and prophets in the Spirit; ⁶ to be specific, that the Gentiles are fellow heirs [Greek: sugklāronomos] and fellow members of the body, and fellow partakers of the promise in Christ Jesus through the gospel.

*QUESTION 6: In light of the parallel between 1 Peter 3:7 and Ephesians 3:6, what do you think Peter means when he calls women "fellow heirs" with men? And what does this imply about how women should be treated?

We too are children of God and will inherit the kingdom of God.

They should be treated with honor (not that submitting is taking aware their honor)

DAY 4: MINISTERING EQUALLY IN THE BODY OF CHRIST

To say that God assigns men and women different roles within the ministry of the local church in no way implies that women have no role to assume. There are an endless number of ministries in this fallen world in which both men and women help people and bring glory to God.

Think over 1 Corinthians 12:14–25.

1 CORINTHIANS 12:14–25

[14] *For the body does not consist of one member but of many.*
[15] *If the foot should say, "Because I am not a hand, I do not belong to the body," that would not make it any less a part of the body.* [16] *And if the ear should say, "Because I am not an eye, I do not belong to the body," that would not make it any less a part of the body.* [17] *If the whole body were an eye, where would be the sense of hearing? If the whole body were an ear, where would be the sense of smell?* [18] *But as it is, God arranged the members in the body, each one of them, as he chose.* [19] *If all were a single member, where would the body be?* [20] *As it is, there are many parts, yet one body.* [21] *The eye cannot say to the hand, "I have no need of you," nor again the head to the feet, "I have no need of you."* [22] *On the contrary, the parts of the body that seem to be weaker are indispensable,* [23] *and on those parts of the body that we think less honorable we bestow the greater honor, and our unpresentable parts are treated with greater modesty,* [24] *which our more presentable parts do not require. But God has so composed the body, giving greater honor to the part that lacked it,* [25] *that there may be no division in the body, but that the members may have the same care for one another.*

*QUESTION 7: How might you use this passage to respond to the following statement: "If women cannot be preaching pastors, then they cannot be as equally valuable as men."

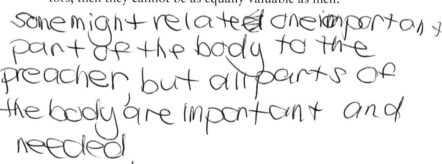

Some might related one important part of the body to the preacher but all parts of the body are important and needed.

Now examine Romans 12:4–8.

ROMANS 12:4–8

> [4] *For as in one body we have many members, and the members do not all have the same function,* [5] *so we, though many, are one body in Christ, and individually members one of another.* [6] *Having gifts that differ according to the grace given to us, let us use them: if prophecy, in proportion to our faith;* [7] *if service, in our serving; the one who teaches, in his teaching;* [8] *the one who exhorts, in his exhortation; the one who contributes, in generosity; the one who leads, with zeal; the one who does acts of mercy, with cheerfulness.*

We would argue that God gives every spiritual gift to both men and women, including the gift of leadership.

QUESTION 8: Is it possible to reconcile Statement A and Statement B? If so, how?

Statement A: "God gives some women the gift of leadership."
Statement B: "God intends only men to be preaching pastors and elders."

Women can have the gift of leadership to lead other women.

DAY 5: EQUAL . . . YET DIFFERENT

In most evangelical feminist literature the claim is made that men and women cannot be truly equal if God has given them different roles in marriage and the church. Piper, however, challenges this assumption:

> Within the equality of personhood and the equality of dignity might there not be some special responsibilities that man has because he is man and that woman has because she is woman? In showing mutual respect and care, might there not be some special ways that a man is to respect a woman and special ways that a woman is to respect a man? Does equality of personhood and mutuality of respect demand sameness of responsibilities or even equal access to all responsibilities? Or did God intend from the beginning that our equality be expressed differently in the way we relate to each other as man and woman?[1]

QUESTION 9: In your opinion, does "equality of personhood" demand "equal access to all responsibilities"? Explain.

No. It is instead showing each other honor and respect in our various and yet all important roles,

This lesson is meant as the first step in the recovery of biblical manhood and womanhood. In the DVD session for this lesson we will listen to John Piper as he gives an overview of the complementarian position and what he takes manhood and womanhood to be.

In this lesson and the following lessons, however, don't forget the fundamental assertion we made in Day 1's study:

A man's call to leadership does not imply that he is thereby superior to a woman; likewise, a woman's call to submission does not imply that she is thereby inferior to a man.

*QUESTION 10: Rephrase this fundamental assertion using your own words.

God calls men to lead women. This does not mean they have more value as women. Women are called to sub mit to men. This does not make them less valuable than men

FURTHER UP AND FURTHER IN

Read John Piper, "A Vision of Biblical Complementarity."[2]

QUESTION 11: According to Piper, what are the two ways in which to commend the biblical vision of manhood and womanhood? Why are both needed?

QUESTION 12: Can a man who is bound to a wheelchair be fully masculine and lead his family? If so, explain how.

Now consider another passage in the Bible that uses the language of "fellow heir": Romans 8:16–17.

ROMANS 8:16–17

> [16] *The Spirit himself bears witness with our spirit that we are children of God,* [17] *and if children, then heirs—heirs of God and fellow heirs with Christ, provided we suffer with him in order that we may also be glorified with him.*

QUESTION 13: Piper declares that Christ is preparing the church to be a "fellow heir" and not a "servant girl" (39). What implications does this have for how a husband ought to lead his wife? Then compare your answer here to your answer to Question 6.

QUESTION 14: Summarize Piper's discussion of a woman's freedom (47–48). How might an evangelical feminist talk about a woman's freedom?

QUESTION 15: According to Piper, what is one sin that is more devastating than the so-called women's movement? Do you agree?

WHILE YOU WATCH THE DVD, TAKE NOTES

The Danvers Statement

1. Adam + Eve equal as persons.
2. Distinctions are ordained by God.
3. Adam's headship ordained by fall.
4. Fall brought about distortions in roles.

Affirmations

5. OT + New points to high value of roles of both genders.
6. Redemption in Christ aims at removing distortions introduced by curse.
7. Christ is the supreme authority + guide. No human goes above Christ's rule.

The Meaning of Masculinity:

8. Men + women should never set aside Biblical criteria for particular ministries.
9. There are so many hurts + pains in this world that no one should ever feel there is no ministry for them.
10. A neglect or denial of these principles will have a devastating affect on our marriages, family + church.

"At the heart of mature masculinity is a sense of benevolent responsibility to <u>lead</u>, <u>provide</u> for, and <u>protect</u> women in ways appropriate to a man's differing relationships."

The Meaning of Femininity:

"At the heart of mature femininity is a freeing disposition to _affirm_, _receive_, and _nurture_ strength and leadership from worthy men in ways appropriate to a woman's differing relationships."

AFTER YOU WATCH THE DVD, DISCUSS WHAT YOU'VE LEARNED

1) Of the ten affirmations in the Danvers Statement, which one do you think is the most important to stress in today's church?

2) As you listened to Piper's definitions of manhood and womanhood, what was the most interesting, curious, or unexpected part of those definitions, in your mind?

3) How might you teach to children what biblical manhood and womanhood are?

AFTER YOU DISCUSS, MAKE APPLICATION

1) What was the most meaningful part of this lesson for you? Was there a sentence, concept, or idea that really struck you? Why? Record your thoughts in the space below.

2) If you are a man, then write your own definition of manhood. You may use Piper's definition of manhood to help you, but put the definition in your own words. Then share your definition of manhood with a male friend of yours. If you are a woman, then write your own definition of womanhood. You may use Piper's definition of womanhood to help you, but put the definition in your own words. Then share your definition of womanhood with a female friend of yours.

NOTES

1. John Piper, "Manhood and Womanhood before Sin," an online sermon at the Desiring God Web site.
2. This essay is available as the first chapter of *Recovering Biblical Manhood and Womanhood* (online for free at the CBMW Web site, www.cbmw.org) or as the short book *What's the Difference?*

LESSON 5
COMPLEMENTARITY AS GOD'S DESIGN IN CREATION
A Companion Study to the What's the Difference? DVD, Session 4

LESSON OBJECTIVES

It is our prayer that after you have finished this lesson . . .

> › You will be able to identify the key interpretive decisions that need to be made in Genesis 2–3 with regard to human sexuality and sexual roles.

> › You will understand how the textual details support the complementarian position.

> › You will be equipped to respond to an egalitarian reading of Genesis 2–3.

BEFORE YOU WATCH THE DVD, STUDY AND PREPARE

DAY 1: WHY IS THE MAN CREATED FIRST?

The previous lessons have focused on setting the stage and introducing the two basic approaches of evangelical feminism (or egalitarianism) and complementarianism. Starting with this lesson, we will begin to examine the key biblical passages regarding manhood and womanhood and hopefully will lay a solid theological foundation for the complementarian position.

In order to do this, we will start with Genesis 2–3. Each day's work in this lesson will seek to answer a question pertaining to these two chapters. The first question is, Why is the man created first?

Study Genesis 2:5–7, 21–22.

GENESIS 2:5–7, 21–22

> [5] When no bush of the field was yet in the land and no small plant of the field had yet sprung up—for the LORD God had not caused it to rain on the land, and there was no man to work the ground, [6] and a mist was going up from the land and was watering the whole face of the ground— [7] then the LORD God formed the man of dust from the ground and breathed into his nostrils the breath of life, and the man became a living creature. . . . [21] So the LORD God caused a deep sleep to fall upon the man, and while he slept took one of his ribs and closed up its place with flesh. [22] And the rib that the LORD God had taken from the man he made into a woman and brought her to the man.

*QUESTION 1: Is there any significance in the fact that God created the man first? Why didn't he create the man and the woman at the same time?

He needed a man to work the ground? He wanted woman to come from man?

Investigate this issue further by reading 1 Timothy 2:12–13.

1 TIMOTHY 2:12–13

> [12] *I do not permit a woman to teach or to exercise authority over a man; rather, she is to remain quiet.* [13] *For Adam was formed first, then Eve.*

QUESTION 2: Did the Apostle Paul see the significance in that fact that God created the man first? If so, of what significance was this fact in his mind?

He saw this as pointing to Adam's leadership and woman's submission to the man.

Now why did God create man and woman in this way? Why did he not create them both simultaneously from the same lump of clay? Would that not have established their equality of personhood more clearly? The answer is that he had already established that beyond all doubt in Genesis 1:27 where it says that both were created in his image.

Now God wants to say something more about the relationship between man and woman. And what he wants to say is that when it comes to their differing responsibilities, there is a "firstness" of responsibility that falls to the man. This is not an issue of superior value. That issue has been settled in Genesis 1:27. It's an issue of a sinless man, in childlike dependence on God, being given a special role or responsibility. God makes him the initial half of the pair to say something about his responsibility in initiating. God makes him lead the way into being to say something about his responsibility of leadership.[1]

DAY 2: WHAT DOES "HELPER" MEAN?

The next thing to reflect on in the creation account of Genesis 2 is the role which God created Eve to fulfill.

Read Genesis 2:18–23.

GENESIS 2:18-23

> [18] Then the LORD God said, "It is not good that the man should be alone; I will make him a _helper_ fit for him." [19] Now out of the ground the LORD God had formed every beast of the field and every bird of the heavens and brought them to the man to see what he would call them. And whatever the man called every living creature, that was its name. [20] The man gave names to all livestock and to the birds of the heavens and to every beast of the field. But for Adam there was not found a helper fit for him. [21] So the LORD God caused a deep sleep to fall upon the man, and while he slept took one of his ribs and closed up its place with flesh. [22] And the rib that the LORD God had taken from the man he made into a woman and brought her to the man. [23] Then the man said, "This at last is bone of my bones and flesh of my flesh; she shall be called Woman, because she was taken out of Man."

A standard egalitarian argument is that because God is called our "helper" in the Bible (see, for example, Psalm 33:20; 70:5; and 115:9), creating Eve as Adam's "helper" doesn't imply anything about her unique role of support and submission.

*QUESTION 3: Using the wider context of Genesis 2, how might you respond to this standard egalitarian argument?

God has a purpose in all he does. He doesn't realize later that Adam needed someone. He knew all along, but had a special plan in when he was going to bring her forth to point to what her role would be in all creation.

QUESTION 4: Read the following six statements about Genesis 2:18–23. Mark a statement with a "T" if it is true and an "F" if it is false.

___T___ It was not good for the man to be alone.

___T___ The man names the animals and the woman.

___F___ A helper for the man is first sought from among the animals.

___F___ Adam finds a helper for himself.

___F___ The woman was formed from the ground like the man was.

___T___ The name "woman" derives from the name "man."

DAY 3: WHY DOES SATAN TEMPT EVE?

Another detail in Genesis 2–3 which you may not have thought about before is the fact that Satan has direct dealings with the woman and not the man. Is there any significance to this observation?

GENESIS 3:1–6

> [1] Now the serpent was more crafty than any other beast of the field that the LORD God had made. He said to the woman, "Did God actually say, 'You shall not eat of any tree in the garden'?" [2] And the woman said to the serpent, "We may eat of the fruit of the trees in the garden, [3] but God said, 'You shall not eat of the fruit of the tree that is in the midst of the garden, neither shall you touch it, lest you die.'" [4] But the serpent said to the woman, "You will not surely die. [5] For God knows that when you eat of it your eyes will be opened, and you will be like God, knowing good and evil." [6] So when the woman saw that the tree was good for food, and that it was a delight to the eyes, and that the tree was to be desired to make one wise, she took of its fruit and ate, and she also gave some to her husband who was with her, and he ate.

*QUESTION 5: Can we say that the serpent tempted the woman because the man was off somewhere else? Underline support for your answer in the passage above.

No, it said in the passage that Adam was with her.

Again, we might be "tempted" to say that Satan's direct dealings with Eve and not Adam is an insignificant detail of the text.

Notice, though, 1 Timothy 2:12–14.

1 TIMOTHY 2:12–14

[12] *I do not permit a woman to teach or to exercise authority over a man; rather, she is to remain quiet.* [13] *For Adam was formed first, then Eve;* [14] *and Adam was not deceived, but the woman was deceived and became a transgressor.*

QUESTION 6: What does verse 14 mean? How does it support Paul's command in verse 12?

It was Eve who was deceived by the snake (but Adam ate as well, so was n't he deceived too). So, b/c she was deceived first, she cannot have authority. ??

Now most commentators in the history of the church have taken this very simply to mean that women are more vulnerable to deception, and therefore should not be given the responsibility of leading and teaching the church. My guess is, from what I have read and experienced, that women are

66

more vulnerable to deception in some kinds of situations and men are more vulnerable to deception in other kinds of situations. . . . The main point is not that the man is unde-ceivable or that the woman is more deceivable.[2]

DAY 4: WHO BEARS PRIMARY ACCOUNTABILITY?

God calls both the man and the woman to account. But observe whom he calls to account *first*.

Study Genesis 3:7–13.

GENESIS 3:7–13

> [7] *Then the eyes of both were opened, and they knew that they were naked. And they sewed fig leaves together and made themselves loincloths.* [8] *And they heard the sound of the LORD God walking in the garden in the cool of the day, and the man and his wife hid themselves from the presence of the LORD God among the trees of the garden.* [9] *But the LORD God called to the man and said to him, "Where are you?"* [10] *And he said, "I heard the sound of you in the garden, and I was afraid, because I was naked, and I hid myself."* [11] *He said, "Who told you that you were naked? Have you eaten of the tree of which I commanded you not to eat?"* [12] *The man said, "The woman whom you gave to be with me, she gave me fruit of the tree, and I ate."* [13] *Then the LORD God said to the woman, "What is this that you have done?" The woman said, "The serpent deceived me, and I ate."*

And then notice what God says to Adam in Genesis 3:17–18.

GENESIS 3:17–18

> [17] *And to Adam he said, "Because you have listened to the voice of your wife and have eaten of the tree of which I commanded you, 'You shall not eat of it,' cursed is the ground because of you; in pain you shall eat of it all the days of your life;* [18] *thorns*

and thistles it shall bring forth for you; and you shall eat the plants of the field."

QUESTION 7: Is there any significance in the difference between Statement A and Statement B?

Statement A: To Adam God said, "Because you have eaten of the tree of which I commanded you, 'You shall not eat of it,' cursed is the ground because of you."

Statement B: To Adam God said, "Because you have listened to the voice of your wife and have eaten of the tree of which I commanded you, 'You shall not eat of it,' cursed is the ground because of you."

In the second, it is pointing to the sin of listening to his wife as the main problem and that is why he is cursed.

Now study Romans 5:12, 14–19, which is a New Testament reflection on sin entering the world.

ROMANS 5:12, 14–19

> [12] *Therefore, just as sin came into the world through one man, and death through sin, and so death spread to all men because all sinned. . . .* [14] *Yet death reigned from Adam to Moses, even over those whose sinning was not like the transgression of Adam, who was a type of the one who was to come.* [15] *But the free gift is not like the trespass. For if many died through one man's trespass, much more have the grace of God and the free gift by the grace of that one man Jesus Christ abounded for many.* [16] *And the free gift is not like the result of that one man's sin. For the judgment following one trespass brought condemnation, but the free gift following many trespasses brought justification.* [17] *For if, because of one man's trespass, death reigned*

through that one man, much more will those who receive the abundance of grace and the free gift of righteousness reign in life through the one man Jesus Christ. [18] Therefore, as one trespass led to condemnation for all men, so one act of righteousness leads to justification and life for all men. [19] For as by the one man's disobedience the many were made sinners, so by the one man's obedience the many will be made righteous.

*QUESTION 8: Underline every reference to Adam or a man in the passage above. Then underline every reference to Eve or a woman. After you finish underlining, record any observations about the significance of this exercise.

All the blame of the sin in the garden was placed upon Adam. Eve and woman is not mentioned here.

DAY 5: ARE ROLE DISTINCTIONS THE RESULT OF THE FALL?

The final question which we will seek to answer is whether male and female role distinctions are a *result* of the fall. Evangelical feminists typically claim that if there were any role distinctions in the Old Testament, they were the consequence of the Fall and are therefore sinful. Egalitarians would argue that in reversing the curse, Jesus has banished any sexual role distinctions in new covenant marriages and in the church.

Read what God says to Eve after the Fall in Genesis 3:16.

GENESIS 3:16

> [16] To the woman he said, "I will surely multiply your pain in childbearing; in pain you shall bring forth children. Your desire shall be for your husband, and he shall rule over you."

QUESTION 9: Respond to the following statement: "God tells Eve that Adam will 'rule over' her as a result of their disobedience to God's command. Therefore, male headship is clearly a sinful result of the Fall, not God's intended design in creation."

It does seem like it's a result of the fall. Maybe it's "discussing a sinful way to rule? But we saw earlier how God had intentions for these roles from the beginning

Study a helpful parallel to Genesis 3:16 one chapter later—Genesis 4:6–7.

GENESIS 3:16

> [16] To the woman he said, "I will surely multiply your pain in childbearing; in pain you shall bring forth children. Your desire [Hebrew: tishukah] shall be for your husband, and he shall rule over you."

GENESIS 4:6–7

> [6] The LORD said to Cain, "Why are you angry, and why has your face fallen? [7] If you do well, will you not be accepted? And if you do not do well, sin is crouching at the door. Its desire [Hebrew: tishukah] is for you, but you must rule over it."

*QUESTION 10: Does this parallel at all illuminate the
meaning of Genesis 3:16? *It sounds more like the result of the fall was that we would desire, as women, to rule, but the right way was the husband was supposed to rule.*

FURTHER UP AND FURTHER IN

Read or listen to "Manhood and Womanhood Before Sin," an
online sermon at the Desiring God Web site.

QUESTION 11: What four observations does Piper make
that indicate that men and women should have different responsibilities?

QUESTION 12: What application does Piper mention at the
end of this sermon?

Read or listen to "Manhood and Womanhood: Conflict and Confusion after the Fall," an online sermon at the Desiring God Web site.

QUESTION 13: According to Piper, what is the essence of corrupted maleness? What is the essence of corrupted femaleness?

QUESTION 14: Record one new thing that you learned by reading or listening to this sermon.

As we contemplate God's design in creation, we must always remember that creation, and marriage, is not about us. It's about him.

God is ultimate and marriage is not. God is the most important Reality; marriage is less important—far less important, infinitely less important. Marriage exists to magnify the truth and worth and beauty and greatness of God; God does not exist to magnify marriage. Until this order is vivid and valued—until it is seen and savored—marriage will not be experienced as a revelation of God's glory but as a rival of God's glory."[3]

This idea is something we will explore more in the next lesson.

QUESTION 15: What is your initial impression of Piper's claim, quoted above?

WHILE YOU WATCH THE DVD, TAKE NOTES

Nine evidences in Genesis 1–5 that man's leadership is an order of creation, not a result of the fall:

#1 The creation of man + woman equally in God's image = leadership function for man,

#2 Man is created first + then woman,

#3 Man is given the moral teaching for governing the garden to pass on to the woman.

#4 Woman was created "from man" and presented as a helper "fit for him."

#5 Man names woman.

#6 The serpent undermines the roles ordained by God and draws Eve + Adam into a deadly role reversal w/ God + each other.

#7 God calls the man to account first, not the woman.

#8 The curse of "desire" —
woman would desire to
rule over man, but he is to
rule over her.

#9 God named man and
woman man.

AFTER YOU WATCH THE DVD, DISCUSS WHAT YOU'VE LEARNED

1) Was there anything confusing to you in Piper's interpretation of Genesis 2 and 3? Did you not understand any of his "nine evidences"?

2) If Genesis 2–3, properly interpreted, teaches that man's leadership is an order of creation and not a result of the fall, is the egalitarian position immediately disproved?

3) How would you summarize, in your own words, what Genesis 2 and 3 teaches us about biblical manhood and womanhood?

AFTER YOU DISCUSS, MAKE APPLICATION

1) What was the most meaningful part of this lesson for you? Was there a sentence, concept, or idea that really struck you? Why? Record your thoughts in the space below.

2) Imagine that you are having a conversation with an unbelieving friend. They want to know why they should care about what the "outdated" book of Genesis says about what it means to be a man or a woman. Plan your response and write down some points below.

NOTES

1. John Piper, "Manhood and Womanhood Before Sin," an online sermon at the Desiring God Web site.

2. John Piper, "Affirming the Goodness of Manhood and Womanhood in All of Life," an online sermon at the Desiring God Web site.

3. John Piper, "The Surpassing Goal: Marriage Lived for the Glory of God," in *Biblical Foundations for Manhood and Womanhood*, ed. Wayne Grudem (Wheaton, IL: Crossway, 2002), 93.

LESSON 6
COMPLEMENTARITY AS GOD'S DESIGN FOR MARRIAGE

A Companion Study to the What's the Difference? DVD, Session 5

LESSON OBJECTIVES

It is our prayer that after you have finished this lesson . . .

> › You will be able to explain how the marriage metaphor is used in the New Testament.
> › You will be able to make some comments on the meaning of Ephesians 5:22–33.
> › You will grasp the beauty of marriage and understand its deepest purpose.

BEFORE YOU WATCH THE DVD, STUDY AND PREPARE

DAY 1: THE MARRIAGE METAPHOR IN THE NEW TESTAMENT

We've seen God's design for complementary, sexual roles within marriage in the book of Genesis. Does this design find an echo in the New Testament? Perhaps the single most important text in the entire Bible about marriage is found in Ephesians 5. Before we get there, however, let's first look at other texts in the New Testament that establish the marriage metaphor.

Consider Matthew 9:14–15 and John 3:27–30.

MATTHEW 9:14–15

14 Then the disciples of John came to him, saying, "Why do we and the Pharisees fast, but your disciples do not fast?" 15 And Jesus said to them, "Can the wedding guests mourn as long as the bridegroom is with them? The days will come when the bridegroom is taken away from them, and then they will fast."

JOHN 3:27–30

27 John answered, "A person cannot receive even one thing unless it is given him from heaven. 28 You yourselves bear me witness, that I said, 'I am not the Christ, but I have been sent before him.' 29 The one who has the bride is the bridegroom. The friend of the bridegroom, who stands and hears him, rejoices greatly at the bridegroom's voice. Therefore this joy of mine is now complete. 30 He must increase, but I must decrease."

QUESTION 1: Though not as clear as the next two passages, what do the two passages above suggest about the marriage metaphor in the New Testament? That is, how is the metaphor used? What truth is being communicated?

Jesus is the bridegroom.
The church is the bride.
Jesus is head of church. Church submits to him. Groom = Christ
Bride = church

Now study 2 Corinthians 11:1–2 and Revelation 19:6–9.

2 CORINTHIANS 11:1–2

*¹ I wish you would bear with me in a little foolishness. Do bear
with me! ² For I feel a divine jealousy for you, since I betrothed
you to one husband, to present you as a pure virgin to Christ.*

REVELATION 19:6–9

*⁶ Then I heard what seemed to be the voice of a great multitude,
like the roar of many waters and like the sound of mighty peals
of thunder, crying out, "Hallelujah! For the Lord our God the
Almighty reigns. ⁷ Let us rejoice and exult and give him the
glory, for the marriage of the Lamb has come, and his Bride has
made herself ready; ⁸ it was granted her to clothe herself with
fine linen, bright and pure"—for the fine linen is the righteous
deeds of the saints. ⁹ And the angel said to me, "Write this:
Blessed are those who are invited to the marriage supper of the
Lamb." And he said to me, "These are the true words of God."*

*QUESTION 2: According to these two passages, who is
the "husband" and who is the "wife"? Why would God use the
marriage metaphor to describe his relationship with his people?

*husband = christ   wife = church
marriage represents a close band
church submits to christ, as wife
submits to husband
wedding represents pure union as we
are pure through christ's blood*

DAY 2: MARRIAGE POINTS TO A DEEPER
REALITY

Now, perhaps, we're in a better position to appreciate Paul's use
of the marriage metaphor in Ephesians 5. The section in Ephesians
5 that deals with marriage is so rich that we'll need to look at it
several times and from different angles. To begin, let's focus on
how the marriage metaphor is used in this passage.

Examine Ephesians 5:22–33.

EPHESIANS 5:22-33

> [22] *Wives, submit to your own husbands, as to the Lord.* [23] *For the husband is the head of the wife even as Christ is the head of the church, his body, and is himself its Savior.* [24] *Now as the church submits to Christ, so also wives should submit in everything to their husbands.* [25] *Husbands, love your wives, as Christ loved the church and gave himself up for her,* [26] *that he might sanctify her, having cleansed her by the washing of water with the word,* [27] *so that he might present the church to himself in splendor, without spot or wrinkle or any such thing, that she might be holy and without blemish.* [28] *In the same way husbands should love their wives as their own bodies. He who loves his wife loves himself.* [29] *For no one ever hated his own flesh, but nourishes and cherishes it, just as Christ does the church,* [30] *because we are members of his body.* [31] *"Therefore a man shall leave his father and mother and hold fast to his wife, and the two shall become one flesh."* [32] *This mystery is profound, and I am saying that it refers to Christ and the church.* [33] *However, let each one of you love his wife as himself, and let the wife see that she respects her husband.*

QUESTION 3: After reading verse 32 in context, what do you think this verse means? What is the mystery about which Paul is speaking?

Here are some comments John Piper has made on Ephesians 5:

It looks as though Paul uses the relationship of human marriage, learned from Genesis 2, to describe and explain the relationship between Christ and the church. But if that were the case, *marriage* would not be a mystery, as Paul calls it in Ephesians 5:32; it would be the clear and obvious thing that explains the mystery of Christ and the church. So there is more to marriage than meets the eye. What is it?

The mystery is this: God did not create the union of Christ and the church after the pattern of human marriage—just the reverse! He created human marriage on the pattern of Christ's relation to the church.[1]

*QUESTION 4: Summarize Piper's comments in your own words. *The intent of marriage is to reflect the glorious relationship between Christ and the church. We are to humbly pursue modeling our marriages off this example.*

DAY 3: MARRIAGE IS ABOUT GOD

The most ultimate thing we can say about marriage is that it exists for God's glory. That is, it exists to display God. Now we see how: Marriage is patterned after Christ's covenant relationship to the church. And therefore the highest meaning and the most ultimate purpose of marriage is to put the covenant relationship of Christ and his church on display. That is why marriage exists. If you are married, that is why you are married.[2]

*QUESTION 5: Do you agree with John Piper's statement (above)? Explain your answer.

yes, I believe our whole lives exist to display God and to make much of him.

If John Piper is right, and marriage is all about God's glory, then it is important to draw out the implications of this for sexual roles.

QUESTION 6: Which of the following statements best expresses your view for how we ought to define sexual roles? Explain your choice.

A) Sexual roles should reflect whatever is thought to be proper and acceptable within each particular culture. Culture is the final standard.

B) Sexual roles should be based solely on competency and desires. If a woman wants to lead her family and she is better qualified than her husband, she should do so.

C) Sexual roles should reflect what the Bible teaches. In this way we can be sure that our sexual roles bring glory to God as he has designed them to do.

D) Sexual roles should be worked out by each family and community. No one has the right to impose their own ideas about sexual roles on someone else.

DAY 4: THE HUSBAND'S ROLE IN MARRIAGE

It is the conviction of this study guide that the Bible must define and regulate our sexual roles. God has designed roles within marriage for the display of his own glory.

Look again at Ephesians 5:22–33.

EPHESIANS 5:22–33

> ²² *Wives, submit to your own husbands, as to the Lord.* ²³ *For the husband is the head of the wife even as Christ is the head of the church, his body, and is himself its Savior.* ²⁴ *Now as the church submits to Christ, so also wives should submit in everything to their husbands.* ²⁵ *Husbands, love your wives, as Christ loved the church and gave himself up for her,* ²⁶ *that he might sanctify her, having cleansed her by the washing of water with the word,* ²⁷ *so that he might present the church to himself in splendor, without spot or wrinkle or any such thing, that she might be holy and without blemish.* ²⁸ *In the same way husbands should love their wives as their own bodies. He who loves his wife loves himself.* ²⁹ *For no one ever hated his own flesh, but nourishes and cherishes it, just as Christ does the church,* ³⁰ *because we are members of his body.* ³¹ *"Therefore a man shall leave his father and mother and hold fast to his wife, and the two shall become one flesh."* ³² *This mystery is profound, and I am saying that it refers to Christ and the church.* ³³ *However, let each one of you love his wife as himself, and let the wife see that she respects her husband.*

*QUESTION 7: Underline all the phrases in this text which describe a husband's role in marriage. Then record a summary of your findings below.

He is the head. He is to love as he loves himself. He is to hold fast to his wife.

QUESTION 8: Is the husband called to imitate Christ or the church within his marriage? Why might this be important?

Christ is the head of the church just as the husband is the head of the family. He is to be the one to take the lead in giving himself up for another.

DAY 5: THE WIFE'S ROLE IN MARRIAGE

We will now repeat the same exercise with regard to a wife's role.

Look once more at Ephesians 5:22–33.

EPHESIANS 5:22–33

> [22] Wives, submit to your own husbands, as to the Lord. [23] For the husband is the head of the wife even as Christ is the head of the church, his body, and is himself its Savior. [24] Now as the church submits to Christ, so also wives should submit in everything to their husbands. [25] Husbands, love your wives, as Christ loved the church and gave himself up for her, [26] that he might sanctify her, having cleansed her by the washing of water with the word, [27] so that he might present the church to himself in splendor, without spot or wrinkle or any such thing, that she might be holy and without blemish. [28] In the same way husbands should love their wives as their own bodies. He who loves his wife loves himself. [29] For no one ever hated his own flesh, but nourishes and cherishes it, just as Christ does the church, [30] because we are members of his body. [31] "Therefore a man shall leave his father and mother and hold fast to his wife, and the two shall become one flesh." [32] This mystery is profound, and I am saying that it refers to Christ and the church. [33] However, let each one of you love his wife as himself, and let the wife see that she respects her husband.

QUESTION 9: Underline all the phrases in this text which describe a wife's role in marriage. Then record a summary of your findings below. She is to submit as she submits to the Lord. She is to also respect her husband.

QUESTION 10: Is the wife called to imitate Christ or the church within her marriage? Why might this be important?

Church- the church submits to the head, to Christ's authority

FURTHER UP AND FURTHER IN

Read "Marriage: A Matrix for Christian Hedonism," an online sermon at the Desiring God Web site.

QUESTION 11: Why does John Piper call Ephesians 5:25–30 a "hedonistic" passage? What does he mean by that word?

QUESTION 12: According to Piper, Ephesians 5:28 is Paul's paraphrase of what? Explain the connection that Piper sees.

QUESTION 13: Are the roles for husbands and wives "arbitrarily assigned"? Why or why not?

Please note that the second half of this chapter anticipates some of the things we will study in later lessons.

QUESTION 14: According to Piper, what cues should a wife take from the church? What cues should a husband take from Christ?

In Lesson 4 we considered the fundamental equality between men and women. In Lesson 5 and in this lesson we began to lay the groundwork for sexual role distinctions. As you think about world history, which message do you think has needed more committed articulation—sexual equality or sexual differentiation? Here are some related reflections by Wayne Grudem:

> For most cultures through most of history the most serious deviation from biblical standards regarding men and women has not been feminism, but harsh and oppressive male chauvinism. It still exists today, not only in some families in the United States, but also in a number of cultures throughout the world. Many non-Christian religions, such as Islam, tragically oppress women and fail to treat them as equals in the image of God.
>
> The first page of the Bible corrects this, in Genesis 1:27, where we find that God created both man and woman in His image. Much of the rest of the Bible goes on to affirm the equal dignity and value of women in the sight of God, and that we must treat one another as equals in God's sight.
>
> This truth has not always been fully recognized, even within the church. I believe that one of God's purposes in this present controversy is to correct some wrongful traditions and some wrongful assumptions of male superiority that have existed within churches and families in the evangelical world.[3]

QUESTION 15: Do you agree with Grudem? Explain why or why not.

WHILE YOU WATCH THE DVD, TAKE NOTES

Prayers from Ephesians

Filled with all the fullness of God

Will we be male and female in heaven?

We will be male and female but there will be no marriage or relations.

The agenda in light of the distortions of sexual roles

men = disengaged or abusive
women = helpless or domineering

Ephesians 5:22–32

verses 22–24

verse 25

Christ gave himself up for
the church.
Men should be dying to
serve their wives!

verses 26–32

You are one flesh. You don't
hurt your own body, so don't do it
to your spouse.

AFTER YOU WATCH THE DVD, DISCUSS WHAT YOU'VE LEARNED

1) Can biblical manhood and womanhood really be that important if there will be no marriage in heaven?

2) How do egalitarians respond to distortions in sexual roles? How should complementarians respond to those distortions?

3) Is this teaching on sexual roles within marriage relevant at all for those who are not married? If so, explain how.

AFTER YOU DISCUSS, MAKE APPLICATION

1) What was the most meaningful part of this lesson for you? Was there a sentence, concept, or idea that really struck you? Why? Record your thoughts in the space below.

2) Imagine that you were asked to share some thoughts about the meaning of marriage at a 50th anniversary party of some dear relatives of yours. What might you share about marriage at this gathering of friends and family? Record your thoughts below and try to incorporate what you've learned in this lesson.

NOTES

1. John Piper, *Desiring God: Meditations of a Christian Hedonist* (Sisters, OR: Multnomah, 2003), 212–213.

2. John Piper, "Staying Married Is Not about Staying in Love, Part 1," an online sermon at the Desiring God Web site.

3. Excerpt taken from Grudem, *Evangelical Feminism and Biblical Truth*, 524.

LESSON 7
DEFINING MALE HEADSHIP ACCORDING TO THE BIBLE

A Companion Study to the What's the Difference? DVD, Session 6

LESSON OBJECTIVES

It is our prayer that after you have finished this lesson . . .

> You will be able to restate Piper's basic definition of headship.

> You will perceive how headship manifests itself in leadership, protection, and provision.

> You will apply the concept of male headship to parenting.

BEFORE YOU WATCH THE DVD, STUDY AND PREPARE

DAY 1: WHAT IS HEADSHIP?

*QUESTION 1: What initial impressions do you have when you hear the word "headship" or the phrase "male headship"? Do you think that your impressions are commonly shared?

leadership, initiative, guidance, seek of wisdom
— not shared by all

Now continue your study of Ephesians 5:22–33.

EPHESIANS 5:22–33

> 22 *Wives, submit to your own husbands, as to the Lord.* 23 *For the husband is the head of the wife even as Christ is the head of the church, his body, and is himself its Savior.* 24 *Now as the church submits to Christ, so also wives should submit in everything to their husbands.* 25 *Husbands, love your wives, as Christ loved the church and gave himself up for her,* 26 *that he might sanctify her, having cleansed her by the washing of water with the word,* 27 *so that he might present the church to himself in splendor, without spot or wrinkle or any such thing, that she might be holy and without blemish.* 28 *In the same way husbands should love their wives as their own bodies. He who loves his wife loves himself.* 29 *For no one ever hated his own flesh, but nourishes and cherishes it, just as Christ does the church,* 30 *because we are members of his body.* 31 *"Therefore a man shall leave his father and mother and hold fast to his wife, and the two shall become one flesh."* 32 *This mystery is profound, and I am saying that it refers to Christ and the church.* 33 *However, let each one of you love his wife as himself, and let the wife see that she respects her husband.*

QUESTION 2: Using this passage above, how would you define or describe Christian "headship"?

serving, loving, caretaker, respectable

DAY 2: A HUSBAND'S LEADERSHIP

We see in Ephesians 5:22–24 that wives are commanded to submit to their husbands, but nowhere do we see husbands commanded to "rule over," "lead," or "govern" their wives.

EPHESIANS 5:22–24

> ^{22} *Wives, submit to your own husbands, as to the Lord.* ^{23} *For the husband is the head of the wife even as Christ is the head of the church, his body, and is himself its Savior.* ^{24} *Now as the church submits to Christ, so also wives should submit in everything to their husbands.*

QUESTION 3: Does this observation imply that husbands do not have a unique responsibility for leadership? If not, then why doesn't this passage give husbands an explicit command to lead?

Now read Mark 10:42–45.

MARK 10:42–45

> ^{42} *And Jesus called them to him and said to them, "You know that those who are considered rulers of the Gentiles lord it over them, and their great ones exercise authority over them.* ^{43} *But it shall not be so among you. But whoever would be great among you must be your servant,* ^{44} *and whoever would be first among you must be slave of all.* ^{45} *For even the Son of Man came not to be served but to serve, and to give his life as a ransom for many."*

*QUESTION 4: How would you respond to an evangelical feminist who claimed that servant leadership, as Jesus teaches it in Mark 10:42–45, nullifies male headship?

It doesn't nullify it. It is what makes it what it is. It's a backward way from seeing it than how the world does.

DAY 3: A HUSBAND'S PROTECTION

Imagine the following scenario:

Two college friends—a man and a woman—are walking back to their dormitories one night after studying together in the library. As they walk through the campus, two men stumble toward them. They appear drunk. These two men start speaking and acting inappropriately toward the young woman.

*QUESTION 5: Which of the following responses seems most natural and fitting? Why?

Response A: The woman speaks up for herself, directly confronting the two drunk men. When the two men become more aggressive, she defends herself and tells her male friend to run to safety.

Response B: The young man intervenes on behalf of his female friend and tells the drunk men to leave her alone. When the drunk men become more aggressive, he puts himself in between them and her and tells her to run to safety.

B = Men were created stronger.

MATTHEW 2:13-15

¹³ *Now when they had departed, behold, an angel of the Lord appeared to Joseph in a dream and said, "Rise, take the child and his mother, and flee to Egypt, and remain there until I tell you, for Herod is about to search for the child, to destroy him."* ¹⁴ *And he rose and took the child and his mother by night and departed to Egypt* ¹⁵ *and remained there until the death of Herod. This was to fulfill what the Lord had spoken by the prophet, "Out of Egypt I called my son."*

QUESTION 6: Why did the angel of the Lord appear to Joseph and not to Mary? Does this passage bear indirect witness to one of a husband's responsibilities?

It does hint toward the husband protecting his wife and family. But, I'm not sure we can base the whole argument on these few verses.

DAY 4: A HUSBAND'S PROVISION
Scan through Ephesians 5:25–30.

EPHESIANS 5:25-30

²⁵ *Husbands, love your wives, as Christ loved the church and gave himself up for her,* ²⁶ *that he might sanctify her, having cleansed her by the washing of water with the word,* ²⁷ *so that he might present the church to himself in splendor, without spot or wrinkle or any such thing, that she might be holy and without blemish.* ²⁸ *In the same way husbands should love their wives as their own bodies. He who loves his wife loves himself.* ²⁹ *For no one ever hated his own flesh, but nourishes and cherishes it, just as Christ does the church,* ³⁰ *because we are members of his body.*

QUESTION 7: According to this passage, what kinds of things ought a husband to provide for his wife?

love, nourishment, cherish

*QUESTION 8: Does it matter who the "breadwinner" is in a Christian family? Is it the husband's responsibility, the wife's, or the responsibility of both equally?

Prov. 31 talks about the woman being industrious at home. It's the husband's responsibility to make sure the family is provided for, but is he the one who is responsible to do the work.

DAY 5: A FATHER TO HIS CHILDREN

Though not an emphasis in this study guide, we will now briefly consider a father's responsibility in parenting his children.

Meditate on Colossians 3:18–21.

COLOSSIANS 3:18–21

[18] *Wives, submit to your husbands, as is fitting in the Lord.*
[19] *Husbands, love your wives, and do not be harsh with them.*
[20] *Children, obey your parents in everything, for this pleases the Lord.* [21] *Fathers, do not provoke your children, lest they become discouraged.*

*QUESTION 9: Are verses 18 and 19 a good summary of what we've learned thus far from Ephesians 5:22–33? Why or why not? How do verses 20 and 21 fit with verses 18 and 19?

yes, it seems to summarize it well.

I don't really see a great connection. Maybe it's just pointing to the need for fathers to be good leaders all around.

Now consider Ephesians 6:1–4.

EPHESIANS 6:1–4

> [1] *Children, obey your parents in the Lord, for this is right.* [2] *"Honor your father and mother" (this is the first commandment with a promise),* [3] *"that it may go well with you and that you may live long in the land."* [4] *Fathers, do not provoke your children to anger, but bring them up in the discipline and instruction of the Lord.*

QUESTION 10: Why is the command to bring up children "in the discipline and instruction of the Lord" given to fathers and not mothers?

It reinforces the leadership role that men are to play in the home.

Here are some of John Piper's thoughts on Ephesians 6:4 and the command "do not provoke your children to anger" in particular:

The father has a leading responsibility in bringing the children up in the discipline and instruction of the Lord. Notice that verse 1 says, "Children obey your *parents*." Both. Not only *father* or only *mother*. But *parents*. But when the focus shifts from the duty of children to the duty of parents, the father is mentioned, not the mother. "*Fathers*, do not provoke your children to anger, but bring them up in the discipline and instruction of the Lord." So my first observation . . . is that in the marriage, fathers have a leading responsibility in bring up the children in the discipline and the instruction of the Lord.

. . . [Paul] warns against provoking anger because anger is the most common emotion of the sinful heart in when it confronts authority. Dad embodies authority. Apart from Christ, the child embodies self-will. And when the two meet, anger flares. A two-year-old throws a tantrum and a teenager slams the door—or worse.

So I think Paul is saying, there is going to be plenty of anger with the best of parenting, so make every effort, without compromising your authority or truth or holiness, to avoid provoking anger. Consciously be there for the child with authority and truth and holiness in ways that try to minimize the response of anger.[1]

FURTHER UP AND FURTHER IN

Read or listen to "Lionhearted and Lamblike: The Christian Husband as Head, Part 1," an online sermon at the Desiring God Web site.

In this sermon, Piper briefly addresses Ephesians 5:21, which some evangelical feminists try to use to refute a man's unique responsibility for leadership.

Read Ephesians 5:18–22.

EPHESIANS 5:18-22

> ¹⁸ *And do not get drunk with wine, for that is debauchery, but be filled with the Spirit,* ¹⁹ *addressing one another in psalms and hymns and spiritual songs, singing and making melody to the Lord with your heart,* ²⁰ *giving thanks always and for everything to God the Father in the name of our Lord Jesus Christ,* ²¹ *submitting to one another out of reverence for Christ.* ²² *Wives, submit to your own husbands, as to the Lord.*

QUESTION 11: How does Piper explain "mutual submission" in this passage?

QUESTION 12: True or False: According to Piper, the roles of husband and wife in marriage are distinct and not arbitrarily assigned, but they can be reversed.

Read or listen to "Lionhearted and Lamblike: The Christian Husband as Head, Part 2," an online sermon at the Desiring God Web site.

QUESTION 13: What rationale does Piper provide for his choice of the sermon title?

QUESTION 14: Describe what Piper means by the following four terms:

Physical Provision

Spiritual Provision

Physical Protection

Spiritual Protection

QUESTION 15: What caution does Piper offer to wives in this sermon?

WHILE YOU WATCH THE DVD, TAKE NOTES

Ephesians 5:33

women — love and respect
your husband
men — love your wife

The book *Love and Respect*

When a wife fails to respect her husband, it causes the husband to not love the wife as much. Then it goes the other way as well.

A definition of headship

"The divine calling of a husband to take primary responsibility for Christ-like, loving, servant **leadership protection** and **provision** the home."

Leadership

Primary responsibility — not sole. Responsibility not rights. Burden-bearer, not boss.

Christ is the head of the church + the leader of the church.

"Note: **servanthood** does not nullify leadership; it defines the **method** of leadership."

Protection

Christ was the savior or protector of the body and died to rescue her.

Provision

Christ nourishes + cherishes the church, just as the man should do for the women.

AFTER YOU WATCH THE DVD, DISCUSS WHAT YOU'VE LEARNED

1) How would you explain Paul's choice of words in Ephesians 5:33?

2) Have you ever seen loving, Christian headship modeled by a husband? If so, what did it look like?

3) Do you think that most Christian wives and women would welcome male leadership when it is carried out in the pattern offered by Christ in Ephesians 5?

AFTER YOU DISCUSS, MAKE APPLICATION

1) What was the most meaningful part of this lesson for you? Was there a sentence, concept, or idea that really struck you? Why? Record your thoughts in the space below.

2) If you are a man, compose a prayer to God asking him to make you into a spiritual leader after the likeness of Christ. Weave some of the language of Ephesians 5 into your prayer. If you are a woman, compose a prayer to God on behalf of a Christian man who is in your life. Humbly ask that God would grow him in mature and godly masculinity.

NOTES

1. These two excerpts are from "Marriage is Meant for Making Children . . . Disciples of Jesus, Part 1 and 2" (respectively). These are online sermons at the Desiring God Web site.

LESSON 8
DEFINING FEMALE SUBMISSION ACCORDING TO THE BIBLE

A Companion Study to the What's the Difference? DVD, Session 7

LESSON OBJECTIVES

It is our prayer that after you have finished this lesson . . .

> You will be able to restate Piper's basic definition of submission.

> You will be able to explain what submission is not.

> You will apply the biblical vision of femininity to motherhood and homemaking.

BEFORE YOU WATCH THE DVD, STUDY AND PREPARE

DAY 1: MANHOOD AND WOMANHOOD IN THE HOME

Before starting our study on biblical femininity and submission, take a few minutes to review the previous lessons, especially Lessons 4–7.

QUESTION 1: As you read over these previous lessons, what do you view as the greatest obstacle to proper male leadership in the home? In other words, what most often keeps Christian men from being Christ-like leaders in their marriages and in their homes?

Pride-talking advantage of their leadership
lack of self confidence- not being a strong enough leader
lack of support from the wife

Consider a scenario in which a man has an eighth-grade education and is married to a woman who is a college graduate. She is smarter than he is, knows more about the Bible, and seems to be more spiritually mature.

***QUESTION 2:** In such a scenario, what should the man do? Should he still be the leader of his home, or should his wife lead the family?

He should, seeking the Lord for guidance,

DAY 2: REVISITING EPHESIANS 5 AND ADDRESSING ABUSE

Let's now turn to Ephesians 5:22–33 yet again.

EPHESIANS 5:22-33

> 22 *Wives, submit to your own husbands, as to the Lord.* 23 *For the husband is the head of the wife even as Christ is the head*

of the church, his body, and is himself its Savior. [24] *Now as the church submits to Christ, so also wives should submit in everything to their husbands.* [25] *Husbands, love your wives, as Christ loved the church and gave himself up for her,* [26] *that he might sanctify her, having cleansed her by the washing of water with the word,* [27] *so that he might present the church to himself in splendor, without spot or wrinkle or any such thing, that she might be holy and without blemish.* [28] *In the same way husbands should love their wives as their own bodies. He who loves his wife loves himself.* [29] *For no one ever hated his own flesh, but nourishes and cherishes it, just as Christ does the church,* [30] *because we are members of his body.* [31] *"Therefore a man shall leave his father and mother and hold fast to his wife, and the two shall become one flesh."* [32] *This mystery is profound, and I am saying that it refers to Christ and the church.* [33] *However, let each one of you love his wife as himself, and let the wife see that she respects her husband.*

QUESTION 3: Underline all of the reasons given for *why* a wife ought to submit to her husband. Then record a summary of your findings below.

He is the head of the family.
We should submit to him as
the church submits to Christ.

It is tragic that some have distorted the loving, sacrificial call to male headship into a warrant for male domination and even abuse. Please allow us to state, as clearly as possible, that domestic abuse is wrong and contradicts everything we've been asserting about the nature of male headship. Female submission does not entail submission to a husband's abuse—whether verbal, emotional, or physical. Here is a portion of CBMW's Statement on Abuse (adopted November 1994):

› We understand abuse to mean the cruel use of power or authority to harm another person emotionally, physically, or sexually.

› We are against all forms of physical, sexual and/or verbal abuse.

› We believe that the biblical teaching on relationships between men and women does not support, but condemns abuse (Prov. 12:18; Eph. 5:25–29; 6:4; Col. 3:18; 1 Tim. 3:3; Titus 1:7–8; 1 Pet. 3:7; 5:3).

› We believe that abuse is sin. It is destructive and evil. Abuse is the hallmark of the devil and is in direct opposition to the purposes of God. Abuse ought not to be tolerated in the Christian community.

› We believe that the Christian community is responsible for the well-being of its members. It has a responsibility to lovingly confront abusers and to protect the abused.

› We believe that both abusers and the abused are in need of emotional and spiritual healing.

› We believe that God extends healing to those who earnestly seek him.

› We are confident of the power of God's healing love to restore relationships fractured by abuse, but we realize that repentance, forgiveness, wholeness, and reconciliation is a process.

› Both abusers and abused are in need of on-going counseling, support, and accountability. In instances where abusers are unrepentant and/or unwilling to make significant steps toward change, we believe that the Christian community must respond with firm discipline of the abuser and advocacy, support and protection of the abused.

› We believe that by the power of God's Spirit, the Christian community can be an instrument of God's love and healing for those involved in abusive relationships and an example of wholeness in a fractured, broken world.[1]

*QUESTION 4: Why might CBMW have issued a statement on abuse?

> some men might take headship to give them an excuse to forcefully lead, some women might think that bic they need to submit that they have to submit to abuse.

DAY 3: ANOTHER KEY PASSAGE ON BIBLICAL FEMININITY

In addition to Ephesians 5:22–33, 1 Peter 3:1–7 is another important passage on biblical femininity and the nature of female submission.

Consider 1 Peter 3:1–7.

1 PETER 3:1–7

[1] *Likewise, wives, be subject to your own husbands, so that even if some do not obey the word, they may be won without a word by the conduct of their wives,* [2] *when they see your respectful and pure conduct.* [3] *Do not let your adorning be external—the braiding of hair and the putting on of gold jewelry, or the clothing you wear—* [4] *but let your adorning be the hidden person*

of the heart with the imperishable beauty of a gentle and quiet spirit, which in God's sight is very precious. [5] *For this is how the holy women who hoped in God used to adorn themselves, by submitting to their own husbands,* [6] *as Sarah obeyed Abraham, calling him lord. And you are her children, if you do good and do not fear anything that is frightening.* [7] *Likewise, husbands, live with your wives in an understanding way, showing honor to the woman as the weaker vessel, since they are heirs with you of the grace of life, so that your prayers may not be hindered.*

QUESTION 5: In order to understand what godly submission is, attempt to compose five statements about what godly submission is *not*. Record your statements below.

1. Godly submission does not include submitting to abuse.

2. Godly submission is not showy.

3. Godly submission does not exclude an active particatory mind and spiritual life.

4. Godly submission is not being weak minded,

5.

Reread 1 Peter 3:7.

*QUESTION 6: What is expected of husbands in view of the fact that the woman is the "weaker vessel"?

understanding, honor

DAY 4: SUBMITTING AS SARAH DID

Focus now on 1 Peter 3:5–6.

1 PETER 3:5–6

> [5] *For this is how the holy women who hoped in God used to adorn themselves, by submitting to their own husbands,* [6] *as Sarah obeyed Abraham, calling him lord. And you are her children, if you do good and do not fear anything that is frightening.*

115

*QUESTION 7: When did Sarah call Abraham "lord"? Using a concordance or cross-references, try to find the specific passage in Genesis. Having found this passage and having read it in context, did you learn anything from the Old Testament context? Record any observations below.

Gen 18:9-12 Paul is saying that Sarah, in her stunned amazement, call him her lord, It's just part of her nature to see him like that,

QUESTION 8: What is the relationship between hoping in God and submission?

Our greatest hope should be in the Lord, not in our husband,

The deepest root of Christian womanhood mentioned in this text is hope in God. "Holy women who *hoped in God*." A Christian woman does not put her hope in her husband, or in getting a husband. She does not put her hope in her looks. She puts her hope in the promises of God. She is described in Proverbs 31:25: "Strength and dignity are her clothing, and she laughs at the time to come." She laughs at everything the future will bring and might bring, because she hopes in God.

She looks away from the troubles and miseries and obstacles of life that seem to make the future bleak, and she focuses her attention on the sovereign power and love of

God who rules in heaven and does on earth whatever he pleases. She knows her Bible, and she knows her theology of the sovereignty of God, and she knows his promise that he will be with her and help her strengthen her no matter what. This is the deep, unshakable root of Christian womanhood. And Peter makes it explicit in verse 5. He is not talking about just any women. He is talking about women with unshakable biblical roots in the sovereign goodness of God—holy women who hope in God.[2]

DAY 5: A MOTHER IN HER HOME

Study Titus 2:1–5 and 1 Timothy 5:9–16.

TITUS 2:1–5

¹ But as for you, teach what accords with sound doctrine. ² Older men are to be sober-minded, dignified, self-controlled, sound in faith, in love, and in steadfastness. ³ Older women likewise are to be reverent in behavior, not slanderers or slaves to much wine. They are to teach what is good, ⁴ and so train the young women to love their husbands and children, ⁵ to be self-controlled, pure, working at home, kind, and submissive to their own husbands, that the word of God may not be reviled.

1 TIMOTHY 5:9–16

⁹ Let a widow be enrolled if she is not less than sixty years of age, having been the wife of one husband, ¹⁰ and having a reputation for good works: if she has brought up children, has shown hospitality, has washed the feet of the saints, has cared for the afflicted, and has devoted herself to every good work. ¹¹ But refuse to enroll younger widows, for when their passions draw them away from Christ, they desire to marry ¹² and so incur condemnation for having abandoned their former faith. ¹³ Besides that, they learn to be idlers, going about from house to house, and not only idlers, but also gossips and busybodies, saying what they should not. [14] *So I would have younger widows marry, bear children, manage their households, and give the adversary no occasion for slander.* [15] *For some have already strayed after Satan.* [16] *If any believing woman has relatives who are widows, let her care for them. Let the church not be burdened, so that it may care for those who are truly widows.*

*QUESTION 9: Underline every word and phrase that describes how a wife should conduct herself within the home. Then summarize your findings below.

submissive, hard-working, caring, kind

Keeping the home is God's assignment to the wife—even down to changing the sheets, doing the laundry, and scrubbing the floors.

. . . Few women realize what great service they are doing for mankind and for the kingdom of Christ when they provide a shelter for the family and good mothering—the foundation on which all else is built. A mother builds something far more magnificent than any cathedral—the dwelling place for an immortal soul (both her child's fleshly tabernacle and his earthly abode). No professional pursuit so uniquely combines the most menial tasks with the most meaningful opportunities.[3]

QUESTION 10: Do you think that homemaking is a challenging "career" for women in which they can express creativity, organization, and leadership? Explain.

Yes, I do. But, I may be a bit biased. I can see how some women may not feel this way.

FURTHER UP AND FURTHER IN

Read or listen to "The Beautiful Faith of Fearless Submission," an online sermon at the Desiring God Web site.

Consider the first word of 1 Peter 3:1—"likewise." To what is a wife's submission compared?

1 PETER 3:1–2

> [1] *Likewise, wives, be subject to your own husbands, so that even if some do not obey the word, they may be won without a word by the conduct of their wives,* [2] *when they see your respectful and pure conduct.*

QUESTION 11: According to Piper, how does 1 Peter 3:1–6 fit into the larger context?

Now look at the next two verses, 1 Peter 3:3–4.

1 PETER 3:3–4

> [3] Do not let your adorning be external—the braiding of hair and the putting on of gold jewelry, or the clothing you wear—[4] but let your adorning be the hidden person of the heart with the imperishable beauty of a gentle and quiet spirit, which in God's sight is very precious.

QUESTION 12: Does 1 Peter 3:3 forbid Christian women from wearing jewelry?

Read or listen to "Honoring the Biblical Call of Motherhood," an online sermon at the Desiring God Web site.

2 TIMOTHY 3:14–15

> [14] But as for you, continue in what you have learned and have firmly believed, knowing from whom you learned it [15] and how from childhood you have been acquainted with the sacred writings, which are able to make you wise for salvation through faith in Christ Jesus.

QUESTION 13: From whom did Timothy learn the Word ("sacred writings")? Why is this significant?

QUESTION 14: What strikes you as you read Bill Piper's tribute to his wife, Ruth?

Homemaking is a vocation often filled with mundane tasks and repetitive chores, most of which are performed in obscurity. It demands a colossal amount of serving and sacrifice. Sometimes between scrubbing toilets or laundering dirty clothes, we can lose sight of the significance of our calling. We look around us and perceive everyone engaged in meaningful work. Everyone, that is, except us. And our vision for working at home begins to flag.

What we need is a biblical perspective. For in God's economy, homemaking is a high and noble calling. Remember our ultimate mission in emulating the Titus 2 lifestyle? By "working at home" we present the gospel as attractive to unbelievers. Our homes can actually be a showcase for the gospel!

When onlookers see us thriving in our role as homemaker, and when they observe the exceptional quality of family life that our efforts produce, this can pique their curiosity. They may want to find out what our secret is!

And our homes can be a place of momentous ministry. They are strategic locations from which we can reach out and extend care to those who don't yet know Christ.[4]

QUESTION 15: Interact with the statement, "A woman's place is in the home." Is this true? What do people mean when they make this statement?

WHILE YOU WATCH THE DVD, TAKE NOTES

Spiritual leadership at home

How does a man deal with a more intellectual, spiritual wife?

Men can spiritually lead in very simple ways-just by initiating, no matter his gifts.

1 Peter 3:1–7

Wife is married to an unbeliever and how she can stay with this man, adornment should not come only from outward appearance,

What submission is *not*

1. Submission does not mean agreeing with everything your husband says.

2. Submission does not mean leaving your brain or your will at the wedding altar.

3. Submission does not mean

4. Submission does not mean putting the will of the husband before the will of Christ.

5. Submission does not mean that the wife gets her spiritual strength mainly from her husband.

6. Submission does not mean acting out of slavish fear toward the husband.

7. Submission does not mean blind or unqualified obedience to the husband,

A definition of submission

inclination + disposition → she's inclined to be supportive, but doesn't always in times of opposition

"Submission is the divine calling of the wife to honor and affirm her husband's *leadership* and help carry it through according to her gifts. Submission is an *inclination* of the will to say 'yes' to the husband's leadership and a *disposition* of the spirit to support his initiatives."

AFTER YOU WATCH THE DVD, DISCUSS WHAT YOU'VE LEARNED

1) Do you think that the scenario John Piper talks about at the beginning of this DVD session is a common one?

2) Which of the seven, false stereotypes Piper mentions about submission have you encountered? Can you think of other things which submission is *not*?

3) How would you explain biblical submission to someone who had strong, negative associations with the word "submission"?

AFTER YOU DISCUSS, MAKE APPLICATION

1) What was the most meaningful part of this lesson for you? Was there a sentence, concept, or idea that really struck you? Why? Record your thoughts in the space below.

2) If you are a woman, compose a prayer to God asking him to make you into a spiritual follower after the likeness of the holy women of old. Weave some of the language of 1 Peter 3 into your prayer. If you are a man, compose a prayer to God on behalf of a Christian woman who is in your life. Humbly ask that God would grow her in mature and godly femininity.

NOTES

1. The full statement is available online at www.cbmw.org/Resources/Articles/Statement-on-Abuse.
2. John Piper, "The Beautiful Faith of Fearless Submission," an online sermon at the Desiring God Web site.
3. Dorothy Patterson, "The High Calling of Wife and Mother in Biblical Perspective," in *Recovering Biblical Manhood and Womanhood*, 366, 367.
4. Carolyn Mahaney, *Feminine Appeal: Seven Virtues of a Godly Wife and Mother* (Wheaton, IL: Crossway, 2004), 112–113.

LESSON 9
ANSWERING OBJECTIONS AND QUESTIONS
A Companion Study to the What's the Difference? DVD,
Session 8

LESSON OBJECTIVES

It is our prayer that after you have finished this lesson . . .

> You will become familiar with some of the most common objections to the complementarian position.

> You will learn to respond to these objections with sound, biblical reasoning.

> You will know how to handle arguments made from experience.

BEFORE YOU WATCH THE DVD, STUDY AND PREPARE

DAY 1: OBJECTIONS? QUESTIONS?

QUESTION 1: Record below one objection or question you have which has not yet been addressed by this study guide or the DVD.

What happens when the other person doesn't come from a biblical worldview?

*QUESTION 2: Record below one objection or question that you think an evangelical feminist would raise in response to what we've studied thus far.

What if they interpret scripture differently than I do?

DAY 2: MUTUAL SUBMISSION

One of the most common responses to the complementarian position, and especially the complementarian interpretation of Ephesians 5:22–33, is an appeal to Ephesians 5:21. Let's look at this verse in context:

EPHESIANS 5:15–23

> [15] Look carefully then how you walk, not as unwise but as wise, [16] making the best use of the time, because the days are evil. [17] Therefore do not be foolish, but understand what the will of the Lord is. [18] And do not get drunk with wine, for that is debauchery, but be filled with the Spirit, [19] addressing one another in psalms and hymns and spiritual songs, singing and making melody to the Lord with your heart, [20] giving thanks always and for everything to God the Father in the name of our Lord Jesus Christ, [21] submitting to one another out of reverence for Christ. [22] Wives, submit to your own husbands, as to the Lord. [23] For the husband is the head of the wife even as Christ is the head of the church, his body, and is himself its Savior.

QUESTION 3: The phrase "submitting to one another out of reverence for Christ" (verse 21) is the final participial phrase in a string of participial phrases. What are these participial phrases modifying? Why might this be significant?

> Be filled with the spirit, we do it all out of strength that comes from the Holy spirit.

*QUESTION 4: How would you respond to an evangelical feminist who asserted that Ephesians 5:21 is the verse which must control our interpretation of all of Ephesians 5:22–33 and that "mutual submission" implies no unique leadership role for men?

> It seems that we should humbly submit to others, But, then it calls out a special submission that the wife must have with the husband.

DAY 3: WHAT DOES "HEAD" MEAN?

Central to our understanding of male leadership is the word "head" that Paul uses repeatedly in Ephesians 5. Evangelical feminists sometimes argue that this word is better translated as "source." Translating the word in this way, they claim, better communicates that Paul did not envision a unique leadership role for men.

Reproduced below are the only four uses of this word in Ephesians. Study these passages and the underlined words below.

EPHESIANS 1:22–23

> [22] And [God] put all things under [Christ's] feet and gave him as head over all things to the church, [23] which is his body, the fullness of him who fills all in all.

EPHESIANS 4:15–16

> [15] Rather, speaking the truth in love, we are to grow up in every way into him who is the head, into Christ, [16] from whom the whole body, joined and held together by every joint with which it is equipped, when each part is working properly, makes the body grow so that it builds itself up in love.

EPHESIANS 5:22–24

> [22] Wives, submit to your own husbands, as to the Lord. [23] For the husband is the head of the wife even as Christ is the head of the church, his body, and is himself its Savior. [24] Now as the church submits to Christ, so also wives should submit in everything to their husbands.

*QUESTION 5: Using these passages, how might you argue for the meaning of head as meaning "a person who is in authority over"?

In the first verse, it talks of christ being put as head over the church. He is the authority in it.

Lesson 9

Another passage which uses the term "head" in a similar context is 1 Corinthians 11:2–3. Consider these verses.

1 CORINTHIANS 11:2–3

> [2] *Now I commend you because you remember me in everything and maintain the traditions even as I delivered them to you.* [3] *But I want you to understand that the head of every man is Christ, the head of a wife is her husband, and the head of Christ is God.*

QUESTION 6: Would it be possible to translate "head" as "source" in this passage? What do you think "head" means in this context?[1]

God was not the head of Christ because they both have always been. therefore, he is the authority over him,

DAY 4: MEN AND WOMEN IN THE WORKPLACE

The focus of this study has been on men's and women's roles in the family. In the next lesson we will consider men's and women's roles in the church. But what about men's and women's roles in the workplace? Does the Bible have anything to say about this?

QUESTION 7: Of the following statements, which best expresses your current understanding of men's and women's roles outside the family and the church? Explain your choice.

A) Women should not be in any kind of leadership position in the workplace that places them in authority over men.

B) There are certain jobs and leadership roles in the workplace that will make godly women uncomfortable in their interactions with men.

C) A woman may have authority over men in the workplace as long as she is not the boss of her husband or any elder in her church.

D) The Bible says nothing about men and women in the workplace and therefore women should feel the freedom to hold any position she can gain by her own competence.

I am guessing that C is the answer, but I think I have always assumed or acted upon D.

*QUESTION 8: Interact with the following statement: "Christians should not dictate what a woman can or cannot do outside of her family and her church since the Bible doesn't have anything to say about sexual roles in the secular realm."

I believe many of the statements in the Bible about this can on should transfer to all of life.

DAY 5: ARGUMENTS FROM EXPERIENCE

Some of the most difficult conversations to have with people are conversations in which someone is arguing from experience.

*QUESTION 9: How would you respond to an evangelical feminist who said the following: "How dare you tell me that God doesn't use women as preachers?! I know some women preachers who have powerful ministries and God has called them to do great things. Are you saying that these women aren't obeying God?"

God has given them gifts and a ministry but can they do that in a position that is not preaching over men.

QUESTION 10: Is it legitimate to support the complementarian position by offering positive, real-life examples of headship and submission? Are all arguments from experience meaningless?

No, I believe it shows the blessings that come from it. Where I might run into difficulty from my experience is when I talk to another personality / career woman,

FURTHER UP AND FURTHER IN

Many egalitarians have argued that the commands for a wife to be submissive toward her husband are not meant to be universal and enduring commands, but only addressed specific problems in their original context. They are therefore not applicable today.

COLOSSIANS 3:18

[18] *Wives, submit to your husbands, as is fitting in the Lord.*

TITUS 2:1, 3–5

[1] *But as for you, teach what accords with sound doctrine. . . .* [3] *Older women . . . are to teach what is good,* [4] *and so train the young women to love their husbands and children,* [5] *to be self-controlled, pure, working at home, kind, and submissive to their own husbands, that the word of God may not be reviled.*

QUESTION 11: How might these passages (and the italicized phrases in particular) support the idea that a wife's submission wasn't only intended for Paul's original audiences?

Skim John Piper and Wayne Grudem, "An Overview of Central Concerns."[2]

Since this is a more lengthy assignment, we do not necessarily expect you to read every question and answer slowly and carefully. If you want, you may choose to skim through this essay, reading every question and then only reading those answers to the questions that interest you.

QUESTION 12: Summarize one question and answer that you found particularly helpful.

QUESTION 13: Summarize one question and answer that confuses you or leaves you with remaining questions.

QUESTION 14: Summarize one question and answer that you could see yourself drawing upon when in a conversation with an evangelical feminist.

QUESTION 15: Turn back to Question 1. What objection or question did you record there? Did John Piper and Wayne Grudem address your objection or question in this essay?

WHILE YOU WATCH THE DVD, TAKE NOTES

Objections

What if the wife is more competent?
Mutual submission?

What about mutual submission?

"Mutual submission doesn't mean that both partners must submit *in* exactly the same *ways*—that's the key that unlocks the seeming problem."

Does "head" really mean leader? What about "source"?

Wayne Grudem has looked at many resources and seen that head does not mean source.

What about the marketplace?

Personal vs. Non-Personal and Directive vs. Non-Directive

AFTER YOU WATCH THE DVD, DISCUSS WHAT YOU'VE LEARNED

1) In your mind, what is the most formidable objection that evangelical feminists can make to the complementarian view? How do complementarians respond to this objection?

2) Did you find Piper's grid of personal/non-personal and directive/non-directive to be helpful? Did Piper change your thinking on this issue? Explain.

3) In light of Piper's discussion of appropriate roles for women, do you think that a woman being the President of the United States would be a violation of her femininity?

AFTER YOU DISCUSS, MAKE APPLICATION

1) What was the most meaningful part of this lesson for you? Was there a sentence, concept, or idea that really struck you? Why? Record your thoughts in the space below.

2) Sexual differences are part of God's design in creation. Therefore, to some degree, they will always find an echo in the human heart.

3) Think of one way in which you can make the truthfulness and beauty of God's design for manhood and womanhood made known outside your family and church. After thinking creatively, record that idea below.

NOTES

1. The difficult text of 1 Corinthians 11:2–16 is not addressed in the DVD. If you have questions about this passage, we would recommend that you consult Thomas Schreiner, "Head Coverings, Prophecies, and the Trinity," which is a chapter in *Recovering Biblical Manhood and Womanhood*.

2. This essay is available as the second chapter of *Recovering Biblical Manhood and Womanhood* (online for free at the CBMW Web site) or as the short book, *50 Crucial Questions About Manhood and Womanhood*.

LESSON 10
MALE LEADERSHIP IN THE CHURCH

A Companion Study to the What's the Difference? DVD, Session 9

LESSON OBJECTIVES

It is our prayer that after you have finished this lesson . . .

> › You will perceive the connection between male leadership in the family and male leadership in the church.

> › You will be able to defend the idea that only men should be elders in the church.

> › You will be able to give reasonable interpretations of 1 Timothy 2:15 and 1 Corinthians 14:34.

BEFORE YOU WATCH THE DVD, STUDY AND PREPARE

DAY 1: LEADING THE HOUSEHOLD OF GOD

This lesson and the next will now explore how complementarianism expresses itself in the church. We start by investigating the connection between the family and the family of God.

139

Examine 1 Timothy 3:14–15 and 5:1–2.

1 TIMOTHY 3:14–15

[14] I hope to come to you soon, but I am writing these things to you so that, [15] if I delay, you may know how one ought to behave in the household of God, which is the church of the living God, a pillar and buttress of the truth.

1 TIMOTHY 5:1–2

[1] Do not rebuke an older man but encourage him as you would a father, younger men as brothers, [2] older women as mothers, younger women as sisters, in all purity.

QUESTION 1: Both of these texts describe the church using a common metaphor. Underline instances of that metaphor. How might the use of this metaphor relate to sexual roles?

Roles of the family carry into the church.

The next passage, 1 Timothy 3:1–5, lays out the qualifications for an elder.

1 TIMOTHY 3:1–5

[1] The saying is trustworthy: If anyone aspires to the office of overseer, he desires a noble task. [2] Therefore an overseer must be above reproach, the husband of one wife, sober-minded, self-controlled, respectable, hospitable, able to teach, [3] not a drunkard, not violent but gentle, not quarrelsome, not a lover of money. [4] He must manage his own household well, with all

dignity keeping his children submissive, [5] for if someone does not know how to manage his own household, how will he care for God's church?

*QUESTION 2: How does the logic of this verse connect male leadership in the home to male leadership in the church?

If he is able to lead his family well, he will be able to lead the church well.

DAY 2: CAN WOMEN BE ELDERS?

One of the questions which every church must answer is whether or not to permit women to be elders in the church. There is no middle ground on this question—either women are permitted to be elders or they are not.

Study the qualifications for elders again in 1 Timothy 3:1–3 and Titus 1:5–8.

1 TIMOTHY 3:1–3

[1] *The saying is trustworthy: If anyone aspires to the office of overseer, he desires a noble task.* [2] *Therefore an overseer must be above reproach, the husband of one wife, sober-minded, self-controlled, respectable, hospitable, able to teach,* [3] *not a drunkard, not violent but gentle, not quarrelsome, not a lover of money.*

TITUS 1:5–8

[5] *This is why I left you in Crete, so that you might put what remained into order, and appoint elders in every town as I*

directed you— [6] *if anyone is above reproach, the husband of one wife, and his children are believers and not open to the charge of debauchery or insubordination.* [7] *For an overseer, as God's steward, must be above reproach. He must not be arrogant or quick-tempered or a drunkard or violent or greedy for gain,* [8] *but hospitable, a lover of good, self-controlled, upright, holy, and disciplined.*

*QUESTION 3: What is meant by this qualification, "the husband of one wife"? Would this qualification exclude women from eldership?

I think it would.

QUESTION 4: Would it be consistent to affirm complementary roles for men and women in the family, but no role distinctions in the church?

No, it would not be consistent. When it comes to spiritual roles, especially, men should lead.

DAY 3: A STRAIGHTFORWARD READING OF 1 TIMOTHY 2

One of the most important passages in the debate about whether women may be elders is obviously 1 Timothy 2:12–14. Before we look at this passage, however, let's briefly consider 1 Timothy

2:11. We will compare it to verses that appear at the beginning of the chapter.

1 TIMOTHY 2:1–2

> [1] *First of all, then, I urge that supplications, prayers, intercessions, and thanksgivings be made for all people,* [2] *for kings and all who are in* high positions, *that we may lead a peaceful and quiet [Greek: hāsuchios] life, godly and dignified in every way.*

quiet, not silent

1 TIMOTHY 2:11 → *in connection w/ acting*

> [11] *Let a woman learn quietly [Greek: hāsuchia] with all submissiveness.*

QUESTION 5: Does the parallel between 1 Timothy 2:2 and 2:11 suggest anything about how a woman ought to act toward authority?

With a quiet spirit + submission

So what sort of quietness does Paul have in mind? It's the kind of quietness that respects and honors the leadership of the men God has called to oversee the church. Verse 11 says that the quietness is "in all submissiveness," and verse 12 says the quietness is the opposite of "authority over men," and so the point is not whether a woman says nothing, but whether she is submissive and whether she supports the authority of the men God has called to oversee the church. Quietness means not speaking in a way that compromises that authority.[1]

Now let's consider 1 Timothy 2:11–14.

1 TIMOTHY 2:11–14

[11] *Let a woman learn quietly with all submissiveness.* [12] *I do not permit a woman to teach or to exercise authority over a man; rather, she is to remain quiet.* [13] *For Adam was formed first, then Eve;* [14] *and Adam was not deceived, but the woman was deceived and became a transgressor.*

*QUESTION 6: Review your answers to Questions 2 and 6 in Lesson 5. Then respond to the following objection: "Paul's command in 1 Timothy 2:12 was motivated by certain circumstances in the Ephesian church. Since uneducated women were teaching heresy there, Paul instructs them not to teach or to use inappropriate power. But we should not understand Paul's command to that specific church to be binding on us today."

DAY 4: 1 TIMOTHY 2:15

One of the more difficult verses to interpret in this debate is 1 Timothy 2:15. Since this verse is not addressed in the DVD, we thought that we might include some discussion of it here.

Study 1 Timothy 2:15 in context.

1 TIMOTHY 2:12–15

[12] *I do not permit a woman to teach or to exercise authority over a man; rather, she is to remain quiet.* [13] *For Adam was formed first, then Eve;* [14] *and Adam was not deceived, but the woman*

was deceived and became a transgressor. [15] Yet she will be saved through childbearing—if they continue in faith and love and holiness, with self-control.

Now study an interesting parallel passage—1 Timothy 5:14–15.

1 TIMOTHY 5:14–15

[14] So I would have younger widows marry, bear children, manage their households, and give the adversary no occasion for slander. [15] For some have already strayed after Satan.

*QUESTION 7: After studying 1 Timothy 2:12–15 and 5:14–15, do you have any idea what 1 Timothy 2:15 might mean?

Here is one possible explanation of 1 Timothy 2:15, found in the book *Recovering Biblical Manhood and Womanhood.*

We think it is preferable to view verse 15 as designating the circumstances in which Christian women will experience their salvation—in maintaining as priorities those key roles that Paul, in keeping with Scripture elsewhere, highlights: being faithful, helpful wives, raising children to love and reverence God, managing the household. This is not to say, of course, that women cannot be saved unless they bear children. The women with whom Paul is concerned in this paragraph are all almost certainly married, so that he can mention one central role—bearing and raising children—as a way of designating appropriate female roles generally. Probably Paul makes this point because the false teachers were claiming that women could *really* experience what God had for them only if they abandoned the home and became actively involved in teaching and leadership roles in the church. . . . Against the attempt of the false teachers to get the women in Ephesus to adopt "libertarian," unbiblical attitudes and behavior, Paul reaffirms the Biblical model of the Christian woman adorned with good works rather than with outward, seductive trappings, learning quietly and submissively, refraining from taking positions of authority over men, giving attention to those roles to which God has especially called women.[2]

QUESTION 8: Summarize Moo's interpretation of 1 Timothy 2:15 in your own words. Does his interpretation strike you as plausible?

Her role, following after the Lord, is in serving her family. Great worth is there — not worth only leading men.

DAY 5: SHOULD WOMEN BE SILENT?

Another difficult passage not directly discussed in the DVD is 1 Corinthians 14:29–35. Does this passage teach that women should be silent in church?

Compare 1 Corinthians 11:4–5 with 14:33–35.

1 CORINTHIANS 11:4–5

⁴ Every man who prays or prophesies with his head covered dishonors his head, ⁵ but every wife who prays or prophesies with her head uncovered dishonors her head, since it is the same as if her head were shaven.

1 CORINTHIANS 14:33–35

³³ For God is not a God of confusion but of peace. As in all the churches of the saints, ³⁴ the women should keep silent in the churches. For they are not permitted to speak, but should be in submission, as the Law also says. ³⁵ If there is anything they desire to learn, let them ask their husbands at home. For it is shameful for a woman to speak in church.

QUESTION 9: Is there an apparent problem or contradiction here? If so, what is it?

There are directions for women of how to pray + prophesy in the church, but then it says that they shouldn't speak in church

In resolving this tension, we would suggest looking at 1 Corinthians 14:29–35 in a different way.

1 CORINTHIANS 14:29–35

²⁹ Let two or three prophets speak,

                  and let the others weigh what is said.

³⁰ If a revelation is made to another sitting there, let the first be silent. ³¹ For you can all prophesy one by one, so that all may learn and all be encouraged, ³² and the spirits of

prophets are subject to prophets.
[33] *For God is not a God of confusion but of peace.*

> *As in all the churches of the saints,* [34] *the women should keep silent in the churches. For they are not permitted to speak, but should be in submission, as the Law also says.* [35] *If there is anything they desire to learn, let them ask their husbands at home. For it is shameful for a woman to speak in church.*

*QUESTION 10: How might this visual layout provide insight into the structure of the passage and its interpretation?

Women may prophesie, but not weigh the prophesy, b/c that is showing authority over men.

Here is another explanation taken from *Recovering Biblical Manhood and Womanhood*:

Paul has just been requiring that the church in Corinth carefully weigh the prophecies presented to it. Women, of course, may participate in such prophesying; that was established in chapter 11. Paul's point here, however, is that they may *not* participate in the oral weighing of such prophecies. That is not permitted in any of the churches. In that connection, they are not allowed to speak—"as the law says." . . . More broadly, a strong case can be made for the view that Paul refused to permit any woman to enjoy a church-recognized teaching authority over men, and the careful weighing of prophecies falls under that magisterial function.[3]

FURTHER UP AND FURTHER IN

Read or listen to "Manhood, Womanhood, and the Freedom to Minister," an online sermon at the Desiring God Web site.

QUESTION 11: How does the review in the beginning of the sermon relate to what follows?

QUESTION 12: According to John Piper, what do "teach" and "authority" mean in 1 Timothy 2:12?

Read or listen to "Affirming the Goodness of Manhood and Womanhood in All of Life," an online sermon at the Desiring God Web site.

QUESTION 13: What are the two reasons that Paul gives for his command in 1 Timothy 2:12? How does Piper explain each reason?

QUESTION 14: What word does John Piper have for singles? How does this relate to what we've been studying?

Another argument made for male leadership in the church is Jesus' choice of apostles. Wayne Grudem explains:

> If Jesus had wanted to establish a truly egalitarian church, He could easily have chosen six men and six women to be apostles, and there would be no room for argument. While some people object that it would have been culturally offensive for Him to do this, if it had been Christ's intention for His church, then He would have done it, for He never hesitated to do culturally unpopular things when they were morally right.
>
> But Jesus did not choose six men and six women as apostles. He chose twelve men. These twelve apostles, under Jesus Christ as the head of the church, have the positions of highest authority in the church throughout its history. And they are all men.[5]

QUESTION 15: Do you agree with Grudem that the choice of twelve male apostles is significant? Explain your reasoning.

WHILE YOU WATCH THE DVD, TAKE NOTES

1 Timothy 2:1-2, 8-15 "quiet" = submissive, not domineering, not rowdy

lead a ⮌ tranquil + quiet life

doesn't mean she can't talk

Are women more gullible than men?

83% of serious crimes are committed by men in the U.S

What kind of teaching should women not do?

"teaching or exercising authority" don't teach over a man women should not be elders, but they can be deacons

A side bar on ministry

To be told "not an elder" doesn't mean "not a minister"

Six thoughts on men and women in ministry

1. All Christians are ministers for the kingdom.

2. Ministry is the use of grace God gives to all.

3. All spiritual gifts are given to women — but being a woman or a man may shape where + how you use them.

4. Pastor / elder / is for men, overseer

5. Elders should be men, women can be deacons.

6. Ministry is not just among the clergy. The whole function of the church is ministry.

AFTER YOU WATCH THE DVD, DISCUSS WHAT YOU'VE LEARNED

1) Did you find Piper's discussion of male and female strengths and weaknesses to be persuasive? Explain.

He said that if you list all of womens strengths + weaknesses and all of men's as well, they would tally to be the same

2) Interact with this statement: "Women should be encouraged to use their teaching gifts within the church."

3) Do complementarians discourage women from serving and ministering within the body of Christ?

AFTER YOU DISCUSS, MAKE APPLICATION

1) What was the most meaningful part of this lesson for you? Was there a sentence, concept, or idea that really struck you? Why? Record your thoughts in the space below.

2) Try to list *every* Christian ministry that you could realistically join, given the constraints of your time and location. Do you have options in ministry? Then share this list with someone else in your church. Can the two of you think of any more? Finish by praying through this list and asking God if he would have you redirect your time, resources, or energy into one or more of these ministries.

NOTES

1. John Piper, "Manhood, Womanhood, and the Freedom to Minister," an online sermon at the Desiring God Web site.

2. Douglas Moo, "What Does It Mean Not to Teach or Have Authority Over Men? 1 Timothy 2:11–15," in *Recovering Biblical Manhood and Womanhood*, 192.

3. D. A. Carson, "'Silent in the Churches': On the Role of Women in 1 Corinthians 14:33b-36," in *Recovering Biblical Manhood and Womanhood*, 151–152.

4. Wayne Grudem, *Evangelical Feminism and Biblical Truth*, 81.

LESSON 11
MEN AND WOMEN IN MINISTRY FOR THE GLORY OF GOD

A Companion Study to the What's the Difference? DVD, Session 10

LESSON OBJECTIVES

It is our prayer that after you have finished this lesson . . .

> You will see how the doctrine of the Trinity is related to sexual roles.

> You will think about the stance or posture complementarians should assume in this debate.

> You will be motivated to minister to the glory of God, whether you are a male or a female.

BEFORE YOU WATCH THE DVD, STUDY AND PREPARE

DAY 1: ROLE DISTINCTIONS IN THE TRINITY

One of contentions of this study guide has been that the topic of manhood and womanhood is tied up with biblical authority. In this day's study we will see that it is also tied up with the doctrine of the Trinity.

Carefully work through John 14:28–31; Acts 2:32–33; and 1 Corinthians 15:22–28, noting how these passages describe Jesus' relationship to the Father.

JOHN 14:28–31

> [28] *You heard me say to you, "I am going away, and I will come to you." If you loved me, you would have rejoiced, because I am going to the Father, for the Father is greater than I.* [29] *And now I have told you before it takes place, so that when it does take place you may believe.* [30] *I will no longer talk much with you, for the ruler of this world is coming. He has no claim on me,* [31] *but I do as the Father has commanded me, so that the world may know that I love the Father. Rise, let us go from here.*

ACTS 2:32–33

> [32] *This Jesus God raised up, and of that we all are witnesses.* [33] *Being therefore exalted at the right hand of God, and having received from the Father the promise of the Holy Spirit, he has poured out this that you yourselves are seeing and hearing.*

1 CORINTHIANS 15:22–28

> [22] *For as in Adam all die, so also in Christ shall all be made alive.* [23] *But each in his own order: Christ the firstfruits, then at his coming those who belong to Christ.* [24] *Then comes the end, when he delivers the kingdom to God the Father after destroying every rule and every authority and power.* [25] *For he must reign until he has put all his enemies under his feet.* [26] *The last enemy to be destroyed is death.* [27] *For "God has put all things in subjection under his feet." But when it says, "all things are put in subjection," it is plain that he is excepted who put all things in subjection under him.* [28] *When all things are subjected*

to him, then the Son himself will also be subjected to him who put all things in subjection under him, that God may be all in all.

QUESTION 1: Would it be biblically accurate to say that the Son "submits" to the Father? If so, should we say that there is "mutual submission" within the Trinity? Explain.

It doesn't seem that there is mutual submission. It just seems like Jesus submits to God.

The importance of roles within the Trinity becomes apparent as we meditate again on 1 Corinthians 11:3.

1 CORINTHIANS 11:3

³ *But I want you to understand that the head of every man is Christ, the head of a wife is her husband, and the head of Christ is God.*

Wayne Grudem explains why the phrase "the head of Christ is God" is important in the debate:

> [In 1 Corinthians 11:3] Paul says that, just as in the Trinity the Father is the leader and has authority over the Son, so in marriage the husband is the leader and has authority over his wife. The remarkable thing is that the parallel with the Trinity proves that it is possible to have *equality in being but difference in roles.* This then disproves the evangelical feminist argument that "if you have different roles in marriage, then men and women are not equal in value." It also disproves the corresponding argument, "If men and women are equal in value, then you can't have different roles in

marriage." In response to those arguments, the doctrine of the Trinity proves that you can have both equality and differences.

*QUESTION 2: Working from 1 Corinthians 11:3, draw a diagram that represents the chain of authority in the universe. Fill in the diagram with notes that explain what authority and submission look like in each relationship.

DAY 2: THE GALATIANS 3:28 STEAMROLLER

We now return to a verse which evangelical feminists use as a building block for their view of sexual roles.

GALATIANS 3:26–28

> [26] *. . . for in Christ Jesus you are all sons of God, through faith.* [27] *For as many of you as were baptized into Christ have put on Christ.* [28] *There is neither Jew nor Greek, there is neither slave nor free, there is no male and female, for you are all one in Christ Jesus.*

Here is what one evangelical feminist has argued in light of this passage:

The most plausible, straightforward reading of Galatians 3:26–28 is that it is an acknowledgement of the fundamental spiritual equality of all categories of people, and a denial of the relevance of gender, race, or social class to the assignment of spiritual roles and privileges.[2]

*QUESTION 3: How might you respond to this egalitarian declaration? (Review your answer to Question 5 in Lesson 4, if necessary.)

God is not saying that gender is irrelevant when it comes to our dealings with each other. Instead it's irrelevant when it comes to our worth and acceptance into the kingdom of heaven.

QUESTION 4: Respond to the following statement: "If Galatians 3:28 makes it clear that there are no significant differences between men and women, Christians should tolerate homosexual relationships."

There are great differences between men + women here on earth! There are just not distinctions in our worth!

DAY 3: OUR MESSAGE TO EVANGELICAL FEMINISTS

Throughout this study guide, we've been arguing that evangelical feminists misinterpret and misuse the Bible in defense of their position. How, therefore, should complementarians respond?

*QUESTION 5: How should complementarians respond to the arguments of evangelical feminists? What should be the tone of our conversation? How serious is this issue?

One major tone should be focused on the difference of roles, not on the differences of worth.

Wayne Grudem describes two different stances that we should avoid in interacting with egalitarians.

> No matter how seriously we differ with other brothers and sisters in Christ, we must continue to treat them with kindness and love. We must continue to report their positions truthfully, without distortion or misrepresentation.
>
> A number of egalitarian leaders today grew up in some extremely strict, harsh, even oppressive environments that taught "male headship" from the Bible but did so without love or without respect and honor for the equal value of women in our churches and before God, and without promoting and honoring the valuable ministries of women in their church. If you support what I say in this book, I ask you, please be careful not to make the same mistakes as others have made and thereby drive other gifted women into the egalitarian camp.
>
> . . . Another ally of egalitarianism is a large group of Christian leaders who believe that the Bible teaches a complementarian position but who lack courage to teach about it or take a stand in favor of it. They are silent, "passive complementarians" who, in the face of relentless egalitarian

pressure to change their organizations, simply give in more and more to appease a viewpoint they privately believe the Bible does not teach.[2]

QUESTION 6: Which of these two stances—harsh and abusive, or cowardly and silent—do you think is more common among complementarians today? What should our stance be?

Cowardly + silent - others desire to be like the world and we don't want to come across as "old fashioned" or a bigot. Affirming but strong

DAY 4: MEN AND WOMEN IN MINISTRY

The Scriptures are filled with examples of men and women in ministry. Here are two examples which describe women engaged in fruitful ministry. We do not view these examples as contradictory to the complementarian view.

Read Judges 4:1–5.

JUDGES 4:1–5

> [1] And the people of Israel again did what was evil in the sight of the LORD after Ehud died. [2] And the LORD sold them into the hand of Jabin king of Canaan, who reigned in Hazor. The commander of his army was Sisera, who lived in Harosheth-hagoyim. [3] Then the people of Israel cried out to the LORD for help, for he had 900 chariots of iron and he oppressed the people of Israel cruelly for twenty years. [4] Now Deborah, a prophetess, the wife of Lappidoth, was judging Israel at that time. [5] She used to sit under the palm of Deborah between Ramah and Bethel in the hill country of Ephraim, and the people of Israel came up to her for judgment.

*QUESTION 7: What ministry did Deborah have in Israel? Does her example contradict the complementarian view?

She was a judge.
Did she give instruction
to men on spiritual matters?

Wayne Grudem cautions us not to be too hasty in using the example of Deborah to support female eldership within the church:

> The book of Judges has many examples of people doing things that we are not to imitate, such as Samson's marriage to a Philistine woman (14:1–4), or his visiting a prostitute (16:1), or Jephthah's foolish vow (11:30–31, 34–39), or the men of Benjamin lying in wait to snatch wives from the women dancing in the feast at Shiloh (21:19–23). The situation at the end of the book is summarized this way: "In those days there was no king in Israel. Everyone did what was right in his own eyes" (21:25).
>
> This is not to deny the grace of God in working through Deborah! Surely the narrative in Judges shows God at work many times in spite of the failures and weaknesses of the people of Israel, and it affirms Deborah as an example of faith, courage, worship, love for God, and godly wisdom. But the unusual nature of Judges should also warn us that it is not a good source for examples of how the New Testament church should be governed. We should be cautious about drawing conclusions for leadership in the New Testament church from a book that primarily describes a breakdown of leadership among the people of God in the Old Testament.[3]

The book of Acts tells us of Aquila and Priscilla, a married couple who explained the Way of God to Apollos.

Inspect Acts 18:1–2, 24–26.

ACTS 18:1–2, 24–26

> [1] *After this Paul left Athens and went to Corinth.* [2] *And he found a Jew named Aquila, a native of Pontus, recently come from Italy with his wife Priscilla, because Claudius had commanded all the Jews to leave Rome. . . .* [24] *Now a Jew named Apollos, a native of Alexandria, came to Ephesus. He was an eloquent man, competent in the Scriptures.* [25] *He had been instructed in the way of the Lord. And being fervent in spirit, he spoke and taught accurately the things concerning Jesus, though he knew only the baptism of John.* [26] *He began to speak boldly in the synagogue, but when Priscilla and Aquila heard him, they took him and explained to him the way of God more accurately.*

QUESTION 8: What ministry did Priscilla and Aquila have in the early church? Does their example contradict the complementarian view?[5]

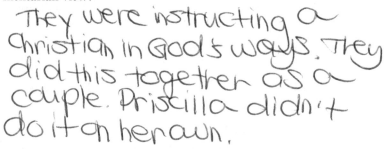

They were instructing a Christian in God's ways. They did this together as a couple. Priscilla didn't do it on her own.

DAY 5: THERE IS MUCH MINISTRY TO BE DONE

In emphasizing the differences between men and women in this study guide, we feel the need to say again that both men and women have indispensable roles to play in displaying God's love in the world.

*QUESTION 9: How might you counsel a woman who was depressed about the biblical teaching on womanhood and didn't feel valued by God or by the church?

Take her through the many opportunities she could have in the church - don't just focus on those she can't.

John Piper has often likened marriage partners to dance partners. In both marriage and dancing, one must lead and the other must follow. Dancing and marriage don't work if both partners (or neither) are leading. And yet, no one consider the dance partner who follows the other's lead to be inferior in any way.

QUESTION 10: Can you think of another analogy in which partners share equal value and dignity but have different roles? Relate your analogy to the mission and glory of God.

- Rowing crew coxin vs. rower
- point guard vs. center in basketball

FURTHER UP AND FURTHER IN

Read or listen to "The Ultimate Meaning of True Womanhood," an online sermon at the Desiring God Web site.

QUESTION 11: Fill in the blank: "My assumption is that wimpy _____ makes wimpy women." Do you agree with Piper?

QUESTION 12: Of the strong women that Piper mentions at the beginning of this message, which one did you find to be the most inspiring? Why?

QUESTION 13: What is God's ultimate purpose in the universe? How does this relate to biblical womanhood?

QUESTION 14: What does Piper say to the married women?

QUESTION 15: What does Piper say to the single women?

WHILE YOU WATCH THE DVD, TAKE NOTES

A final thought on men and women in ministry

Clergy are not the only ones who have an opportunity for a vibrant ministry.

The New Testament elevates women

- *Jesus honored women in his ministry.*
- *Peter confirmed that women would prophesy with men.*
- *Paul worked with women.*
- *Peter extoled women as heirs to the kingdom.*

Galatians 3:27–28

Paul taught that neither manhood nor womanhood is a hindrance to the fullness of Christ.
→ *We are equally baptized into Christ.*

The Influence of Mothers

Why Piper stands by this distinction in role between men and women in ministry

1. b/c the sense seems plain + not complicated

2.

3. No texts contradict Complentarianism,

4. Aim of NT is to redeem sin distorted relationships by removing distortions in headship.

5. What the Bible teaches about completarity, brings great joy!

AFTER YOU WATCH THE DVD, DISCUSS WHAT YOU'VE LEARNED

1) If we were to become more like Jesus in the way we treated women, how would we act? How would we *not* act?

2) What overlap is there between biblical manhood and womanhood and the issue of homosexuality?

3) Of all the biblical arguments for the complementarian view you've encountered in this study guide and in the DVD, which do you consider to be the strongest? How might you present these arguments to those who are skeptical of or opposed to the biblical vision we've presented?

AFTER YOU DISCUSS, MAKE APPLICATION

1) What was the most meaningful part of this lesson for you? Was there a sentence, concept, or idea that really struck you? Why? Record your thoughts in the space below

2) One of the most effective ways of retaining and deepening something you've learned is to teach it to someone else. Identify at least one person with whom you'd like to share what you've learned in this group study. How will you communicate the biblical vision of manhood and womanhood with that person?

NOTES

1. Rebecca Groothius, *Good News for Women: A Biblical Picture of Gender Equality* (Grand Rapids, MI: Baker Book House, 1997), 36.

2. John Piper, *Future Grace* (Sisters, OR: Multnomah, 2003), 261.

3. Grudem, *Evangelical Feminism and Biblical Truth*, 135–136. For a more thorough discussion of Deborah, see Grudem's discussion in this book on pages 131–136.

4. Again, for a more thorough discussion of Priscilla and Aquila, see Grudem, *Evangelical Feminism and Biblical Truth*, 177–180.

LESSON 12
REVIEW AND CONCLUSION

LESSON OBJECTIVES

It is our prayer that after you have finished this lesson . . .

> You will be able to summarize and synthesize what you've learned.
> You will hear what others in your group have learned.
> You will share with others how you have begun to put into practice the biblical vision of manhood and womanhood.

WHAT HAVE YOU LEARNED?

There are no study questions to answer in preparation for this lesson. Instead, spend your time writing a few paragraphs that explain what you've learned in this group study. To help you do this, you may choose to review the notes you've taken in the previous lessons. Then, after you've written down what you've learned, write down some questions that still remain in your mind about anything addressed in these lessons. Be prepared to share these reflections and questions with the group in the next lesson.

NOTES

Use this space to record anything in the group discussion that you want to remember:

LEADER'S GUIDE

AS THE LEADER OF THIS GROUP STUDY, *it is imperative that you are completely familiar with this study guide* and with the *What's the Difference?* DVD set. Therefore, it is our strong recommendation that you (1) read and understand the introduction, (2) skim each lesson, surveying its layout and content, and (3) read the entire Leader's Guide *before* you begin the group study and distribute the study guides. As you review this Leader's Guide, keep in mind that the material here is only a recommendation. As the leader of the study, feel free to adapt this study guide to your situation and context.

BEFORE LESSON 1

Before the first lesson, you will need to know approximately how many participants you will have in your group study. *Each participant will need his or her own study guide!* Therefore, be sure to order enough study guides. You will distribute these study guides at the beginning of the first lesson.

It is also our strong recommendation that you, as the leader, familiarize yourself with this study guide and the *What's the Difference?* DVD set in order to answer any questions that might arise and also to ensure that each group session runs smoothly and maximizes the learning of the participants. It is not necessary for you to preview *What's the Difference?* in its entirety—although it certainly wouldn't hurt!—but you should be prepared to navigate your way through each DVD menu.

DURING LESSON 1

Each lesson is designed for a one-hour group session. Lessons 2–12 require preparatory work from the participant before this group session. Lesson 1, however, requires no preparation on the part of the participant.

The following schedule is how we suggest that you use the first hour of your group study:

INTRODUCTION TO THE STUDY GUIDE (10 MINUTES)

Introduce this study guide and the *What's the Difference?* DVD. Share with the group why you chose to lead the group study using these resources. Inform your group of the commitment that this study will require and motivate them to work hard. Pray for the twelve-week study, asking God for the grace you will need. Then distribute one study guide to each participant. You may read the Introduction aloud, if you want, or you may immediately turn the group to Lesson 1 (starting on page 13 of this study guide).

PERSONAL INTRODUCTIONS (15 MINUTES)

Since group discussion will be an integral part of this guided study, it is crucial that each participant feels welcome and safe. The goal of each lesson is for every participant to contribute to the discussion in some way. Therefore, during these 15 minutes, have participants introduce themselves. You may choose to use the questions listed in the section entitled, *"About Yourself,"* or you may ask questions of your own choosing.

DISCUSSION (25 MINUTES)

Transition from the time of introductions to the discussion questions, listed under the heading "A Preview of *What's the Difference?*" Invite everyone in the class to respond to these questions, but don't let the discussion become too involved. These questions are designed to spark interest and generate questions. The aim is not to come to definitive answers yet.

REVIEW AND CLOSING (10 MINUTES)

End the group session by reviewing Lesson 2 with the group participants and informing them of the preparation that they must do before the group meets again. Encourage them to be faithful in preparing for the next lesson. Answer any questions that the group may have and then close in prayer.

BEFORE LESSONS 2–11

As the group leader, you should do all the preparation for each lesson that is required of the group participants, that is, the ten study questions. Furthermore, it is highly recommended that you complete the entire "Further Up and Further In" section. This is not required of the group participants, but it will enrich your preparation and help you to guide and shape the conversation more effectively.

The group leader should also preview the session of *What's the Difference?* that will be covered in the next lesson. So, for example, if the group participants are doing the preparatory work for Lesson 3, you should preview *What's the Difference?* Session 2, before the group meets and views it. Previewing each session will better equip you to understand the material and answer questions. If you want to pause the DVD in the midst of the session in order to clarify or discuss, previewing the session will allow you to plan where you want to take your pauses.

Finally, you may want to supplement or modify the discussion questions or the application assignment. Please remember that *this study guide is a resource*; any additions or changes you make that better match the study to your particular group are encouraged. As the group leader, your own discernment, creativity, and guidance are invaluable, and you should adapt the material as you see fit.

Plan for about two hours of your own preparation before each lesson!

DURING LESSONS 2–11

Again, let us stress that during Lessons 2–11, you may use the group time in whatever way you desire. The following schedule, however, is what we suggest:

DISCUSSION (15 MINUTES)

Begin your time with prayer. The tone you set in your prayer will likely be impressed upon the group participants: if your prayer is serious and heartfelt, the group participants will be serious about prayer; if your prayer is hasty, sloppy, or a token gesture, the group participants will share this same attitude toward prayer. So model the kind of praying that you desire your students to imitate.

Remember, the blood of Jesus has bought your access to the throne of grace.

After praying, review the preparatory work that the participants completed. How did they answer the questions? Which questions did they find to be the most interesting or the most confusing? What observations or insights can they share with the group? If you would like to review some tips for leading productive discussion, please turn to Appendix B at the end of this study guide.

The group participants will be provided an opportunity to apply what they've learned in Lessons 2–11. As the group leader, you can choose whether it would be appropriate for the group to discuss these assignments during this 15 minute time-slot.

DVD VIEWING (25 MINUTES)[1]

Play the session for *What's the Difference?* that corresponds to the lesson you're studying. You may choose to pause the DVD at crucial points to check for understanding and provide clarification. Or you may choose to watch the DVD without interruption.

DISCUSSION AND CLOSING (20 MINUTES)

Foster discussion on what was taught during John Piper's session. You may do this by first reviewing the DVD notes (under the heading "While You Watch the DVD, Take Notes") and then proceeding to the discussion questions, listed under the heading "After You Watch the DVD, Discuss What You've Learned." These discussion questions are meant to be springboards that launch the group into further and deeper discussion. Don't feel constrained to cover these questions if the group discussion begins to move in other helpful directions.

Close the time by briefly reviewing the application section and the homework that is expected for the next lesson. Pray and dismiss.

BEFORE LESSON 12

It is important that you encourage the group participants to complete the preparatory work for Lesson 12. This assignment invites the participant to reflect on what they've learned and what remaining questions they still have. As the group leader, this would be a helpful assignment for you to complete as well. In addition, you may want to write down the key concepts of this DVD series that you want the group participants to walk away with.

DURING LESSON 12

The group participants are expected to complete a reflection exercise as part of their preparation for Lesson 12. The bulk of the group time during this last lesson should be focused on reviewing and synthesizing what was learned. Encourage each participant to share some recorded thoughts. Attempt to answer any remaining questions that they might have.

To close this last lesson, you might want to spend extended time in prayer. If appropriate, take prayer requests relating to what the participants have learned in these ten weeks, and bring these requests to God.

It would be completely appropriate for you, the group leader, to give a final charge or word of exhortation to end this group study. Speak from your heart and out of the overflow of joy that you have in God.

Please receive our blessing for all you group leaders who choose to use this study guide:

The LORD bless you and keep you; the LORD make his face to shine upon you and be gracious to you; the LORD lift up his countenance upon you and give you peace. (Numbers 6:24–26)

NOTES

1. Twenty-five minutes is only an approximation. Some of the sessions are shorter; some are longer. You may need to budget your group time differently, depending upon which session you are viewing.

APPENDIX A
SIX-SESSION INTENSIVE OPTION

WE UNDERSTAND THAT THERE ARE circumstances which may prohibit a group from devoting twelve sessions to this study. In view of this, we have designed a six-session intensive option for groups that need to complete the material in less time. In the intensive option, the group should meet for two hours each week. Here is our suggestion for how to complete the material in six weeks:

Week 1 Introduction to the Study Guide and Lesson 1
Week 2 Lessons 2 and 3 (DVD Sessions 1 and 2)
Week 3 Lessons 4 and 5 (DVD Sessions 3 and 4)
Week 4 Lessons 6 and 7 (DVD Sessions 5 and 6)
Week 5 Lessons 8 and 9 (DVD Sessions 7 and 8)
Week 6 Lessons 10 and 11 (DVD Sessions 9 and 10)

Notice that we have not included Lesson 12 in the intensive option. Moreover, because each participant is required to complete two lessons per week, it will be necessary to combine the number of "days" within each lesson so that all of the material is covered. Thus, for example, during Week 2 in the intensive option, each participant will complete

> Lesson 2, Days 1 and 2, on the first day;
> Lesson 2, Days 3 and 4, on the second day;
> Lesson 2, Day 5 and Lesson 3, Day 1, on the third day;

> Lesson 3, Days 2 and 3, on the fourth day;

> Lesson 3, Days 4 and 5, on the fifth day.

Because of the amount of material, we recommend that students focus on questions marked with an asterisk (*) first, and then, if time permits, complete the rest of the questions.

APPENDIX B
LEADING PRODUCTIVE DISCUSSIONS

Note: This material has been adapted from curricula produced by The Bethlehem Institute (TBI), a ministry of Bethlehem Baptist Church. It is used by permission.

IT IS OUR CONVICTION THAT the best group leaders foster an environment in their group that engages the participants. Most people learn by solving problems or by working through things that provoke curiosity or concern. Therefore, we discourage you from ever "lecturing" for the entire lesson. Although a group leader will constantly shape conversation, clarifying and correcting as needed, they will probably not talk for the majority of the lesson. This study guide is meant to facilitate an investigation into biblical truth—an investigation that is shared by the group leader and the participants. Therefore, we encourage you to adopt the posture of a "fellow-learner" who invites participation from everyone in the group.

It might surprise you how eager people can be to share what they have learned in preparing for each lesson. Therefore, you should invite participation by asking your group participants to share their discoveries. Here are some of our "tips" on facilitating discussion that is engaging and helpful:

> › Don't be uncomfortable with silence initially. Once the first participant shares their response, others will be likely to join in. But if you cut the silence short by

prompting them, then they are more likely to wait for you to prompt them every time.

> Affirm every answer, if possible, and draw out the participants by asking for clarification. Your aim is to make them feel comfortable sharing their ideas and learning, so be extremely hesitant to "shut down" a group member's contribution or "trump" it with your own. This does not mean, however, that you shouldn't correct false ideas—just do it in a spirit of gentleness and love.

> Don't allow a single person, or group of persons, to dominate the discussion. Involve everyone, if possible, and intentionally invite participation from those who are more reserved or hesitant.

> Labor to show the significance of their study. Emphasize the things that the participants could not have learned without doing the homework.

> Avoid talking too much. The group leader should not monopolize the discussion, but rather guide and shape it. If the group leader does the majority of the talking, the participants will be less likely to interact and engage, and therefore they will not learn as much. Avoid constantly adding the "definitive last word."

> The group leader should feel the freedom to linger on a topic or question if the group demonstrates interest. The group leader should also pursue digressions that are helpful and relevant. There is a balance to this, however: the group leader *should* attempt to cover the material. So avoid the extreme of constantly wandering off topic, but also avoid the extreme of limiting the conversation in a way that squelches curiosity or learning.

> The group leader's passion, or lack of it, is infectious. Therefore, if you demonstrate little enthusiasm for the material, it is almost inevitable that your participants will likewise be bored. But if you have a genuine excite-

ment for what you are studying, and if you truly think Bible study is worthwhile, then your group will be impacted positively. Therefore, it is our recommendation that before you come to the group, you spend enough time working through the homework and praying, so that you can overflow with genuine enthusiasm for the Bible and for God in your group. This point cannot be stressed enough. Delight yourself in God and in his Word!

10/14/10

Kate - Action for Dan to get over depression

Lyndsey - changes at work, review next Friday; stress at work (katie)

Justin - super busy and stressful at work meet his dead lines on time

Kelly (katie's sister) trying to have a baby; stress of baby getting better

Ashley - work is extremely busy,

10/28 Lyndsey - traveling PRAY for ASHLEY

Shanna - cortizone shot, hard year @ school

Kate - aunt w/ cancer going into hospice (Linda + Steve)

Katie - sister's dye test tomorrow
Praise for peace about the birthing process, Justin less busy

Ashley - feeling better, diligence to go to bed earlier, praise for whole family coming for Thanksgiving, still looking for car

11/18

Katie—smooth and safe delivery, patience for waiting, praise things have slowed down for Justin, sister been trying to have baby for two years

Shanna—

12/2/10

Katie B - praise for healthy baby

Lyndsey—Chris away, anxiety while he's gone work is greatly decreasing

Shanna—comfort for Colleen
praise for back feeling okay

Ashley—praise that ultrasound looked good
change to qualify for disability
while gone w/ baby
praise that feeling well

Kate—found a great specialist to talk with
find something! Answers!
Praise for progress in Dan's heart
motivated to action

12/16/10

Katie B.—anxiety about Josie, wisdom for Justin's career, new car?, safe travel to Iowa

Kate S.—praise that tests for Dan went well, wisdom of what steps to take next, praise that Dan is going to see counseling

Shanna—rejuvination during break, a hopeful attitude towards students, strength for the change w/ Mikes job + grad school

Ashley—healing for sickness, praise that Fitsok has been very good to them

⚙ desiringGod

If you would like to further explore the vision of God and life presented in this book, we at Desiring God would love to serve you.
We have hundreds of resources to help you grow in your passion
for Jesus Christ and help you spread that passion to others. At our
website, desiringGod.org, you'll find almost everything John Piper
has written and preached, including more than thirty books. We've
made over twenty-five years of his sermons available free online for
you to read, listen to, download, and in some cases watch.

In addition, you can access hundreds of articles, listen to our daily
internet radio program, find out where John Piper is speaking, learn
about our conferences, discover our God-centered children's curricula, and browse our online store. John Piper receives no royalties
from the books he writes and no compensation from Desiring God.
The funds are all reinvested into our gospel-spreading efforts. DG
also has a whatever-you-can-afford policy, designed for individu-
als with limited discretionary funds. If you'd like more information
about this policy, please contact us at the address or phone number below. We exist to help you treasure Jesus Christ and his gospel
above all things because he is most glorified in you when you are
most satisfied in him. Let us know how we can serve you!

Desiring God
Post Office Box 2901
Minneapolis, Minnesota 55402

888.346.4700
mail@desiringGod.org
www.desiringGod.org

1/13/11

KatieB - peace and help while Justin travels
wisdom for Justin and his job
anxiety about Josie
Josie to sleep longer at night

KatieS - wisdom to know how to help Dan
consistency + discipline in devotions
Dan's uncle has lymphoma

Ashley - feeling stressed about coming baby
Jeff deciding about Hawaii wedd.

1/27/11

Ashley - Jeff's grandma passed away, feeling
very stressed with work right now, ultrasound
went well and she looked good, her dad +
Theresa's grandkid in a bad situation

Me - Praise for responsiveness in Russ, Debbie
Pray for my heart and patience for braces.

KatieS. - patience for the Lord in infertility
Pray that Dan will stay in the small group

KatieB. - anxiety is much better Josie is sleeping
through the night, establishing a routine as
a family

2/10/11 Shanna - Praise for changes in class, jog, lau
KatieB - sister Kelly is stopping all fertility meds, big decis
to make ahead

KatieS - praise for upcoming conversation with
cousin about infertility, Dan's uncle's health,
wisdom for new job option

Ashley - wisdom to know about job, child care, etc

2/24/11 Shanna - wisdom + forgiveness to Maride
KatieB - Praise for good sleep, wisdom to know how
meet Justin halfway, Jeff + Kelly met with adopt
agency, transition back to work, wisdom for a
nanny

Ashley - physical comfort and sleeping, praise for
protection when falling, interview tomorrow
KateS - patience + wisdom w/ Dan, softening of heart